PYTHON

2 BOOKS IN 1:
LEARN PYTHON PROGRAMMING FOR BEGINNERS AND MACHINE LEARNING

WILLARD D. SANDERS

THIS BOOK INCLUDES

BOOK 1:

LEARN PYTHON PROGRAMMING FOR BEGINNERS:

A Beginner's Guide to Comprehending Python. Develop Your Programming Skills and Learn All the Tricks with This Crash Course.

BOOK 2:

PYTHON MACHINE LEARNING

The Complete Beginner's Guide to Deep Learning with Python. Learn How to Use Scikit-Learn and Pandas.

LEARN PYTHON PROGRAMMING
FOR BEGINNERS:

Table of Contents

PYTHON MACHINE LEARNING

Table of Contents

LEARN PYTHON PROGRAMMING FOR BEGINNERS:

A Beginner's Guide to Comprehending Python. Develop Your Programming Skills and Learn All the Tricks with This Crash Course.

WILLARD D. SANDERS

INTRODUCTION

The following chapters of this book will discuss Python as a programming language. Each chapter will take you on an in-depth journey into understanding the Python programming language. This book was written to provide the reader with an understanding of Python. The author of this book has conducted thorough research through sources believed to be reliable to come up with the relevant information on the topic.

Go ahead and read through the entire book, get the knowledge, and be informed about the key things that you need to know about this particular topic. Python is a programming language that is often recommended for beginners to try messing up things and falling in love with programming. One of the major reasons for the widespread popularity of Python is its simplicity and the power of making things done with less code. Even after the entrance of tens of programming languages in the past decade python doesn't lose its charm and we are pretty confident that it is going to stay.

This book is primarily for people who are relatively new to programming and, more specifically, those who want to discover the world of Python. This book will take you through the fundamentals of programming and Python.

CHAPTER 1:

WHAT IS PYTHON

What is Python?

Python is an awesome decision on machine learning for a few reasons. Most importantly, it's a basic dialect at first glance. Regardless of whether you're not acquainted with Python, getting up to speed is snappy if you at any point have utilized some other dialect with C-like grammar.

Second, Python has an incredible network that results in great documentation and inviting and extensive answers in StackOverflow (central!).

Third, coming from the colossal network, there are a lot of valuable libraries for Python (both as "batteries included" an outsider), which take care of essentially any issue that you can have (counting machine learning).

However, here's the caveat: libraries can and do offload the costly computations to the substantially more performant (yet much harder to use) C and C++ are prime examples. There's NumPy, which is a library for numerical calculation. It is composed of C, and it's quick. Therefore, each library out there that includes serious estimations utilizes it—every one of the libraries recorded next utilizes it in some shape. On the off chance that you read NumPy, think quickly.

In this way, you can influence your computer scripts to run essentially as quickly as handwriting them out in a lower level dialect. So, there's truly nothing to stress over with regards to speed and agility.

Python is one of the most important programming languages nowadays, being a general-purpose language.

With this language, you can create a huge and varied amount of applications, because it allows you to create different kinds of applications since it doesn't have a defined purpose.

History and Evolution

Since computers were first invented, many people have had the job to make them more useful. To make this happen, there are a ton of programming tools that have been developed over the years to turn

13

the instructions the computer is given into code that the computer can execute. When this first started, assembly language was the main type. While it did allow you to create programming that was tailored and then optimized for the low memory systems of that time, it was hard to learn, read, and maintain and only a few people could use it.

As computer technology grew and many systems became more complex, the programming languages needed to change as well. Some higher-level languages including Lisp, Cobol, and Fortran were produced to produce punch cards which the computers were able to read and then execute the instructions that were found on the card. Programming with this kind of tool was a lot easier than the languages in the past, allowing more people to write the complex programs they needed.

As time started to go on, there were a lot of improvements that were made to some of the technology that we are working with now, and it has resulted in a lot of better storage methods when it comes to our programs and more. For example, some of those punch cards have been replaced with a type of magnetic tape, and then it was all moved over to work with a disc drive. As these new inventions came out, the tools to work on these programs improved as well.

Basic was one of the first coding languages that was designed to be easy to read through and this one was developed in the 1960s. Then in the 1970s, we saw the introduction of Pascal and C, and these became tools that helped us to get a really simple and structured kind of programming language that would help a programmer to get the efficient code that they want. You will find that the structured languages like these would not have to rely on the go-to statement found in some of the other languages. Instead, these programs would rely on a flow that has features including conditional statements, functions, and loops like we will talk about later in this guidebook. These features were nice because they would allow a new programmer to make their applications with the help of standalone reusable routines, which would then be able to lower the amount of time that it would take to develop the program, and even debug it so that the program would work the way that you would like.

It was in the 1980s when the next big advancement in programming happened This was where C++, and a few other languages, turned into OOP languages, or object-oriented programming languages. There are a number of these that are now available and usable, but they were useful because they helped us to hold onto our information better. While these tools of OOP languages were powerful and had some new capabilities when it came to coding, many times they would be seen as special because they could cut out some of the challenges that came with coding.

As the use and the popularity of computers started to grow, and it became common for more people to use them, it was also an important factor to have a language for programming that was easy to use, one that we can use on a lot of different platforms. Because of this need, the language that we know as Python today was developed.

Python is going to be a general-purpose programming language. Whether you are a beginner or someone who has been in the coding world for some time, you will find that this language is easy to learn while still making sure that there is a lot of power behind it to get those codes done. You can use this for a lot of different purposes, from some general housekeeping tasks for your system to just having fun and making your programs and games. Of course, when you compare this language to some of the others out there, you will also notice that Python is going to have a lot of rules and structures that you must follow to get this to work. No matter what codes you would like to write in Python, you will need to follow the rules and ensure that the compiler is ready to handle it all. The good news is that the rules are pretty simple with this language and you will find that this language is simple, powerful, and compact all in one. As a beginner, it is easier to catch onto this kind of coding language than you think, and before long, and with the help of this guidebook, you will be able to get everything to work the way you would like and will be writing your codes in no time.

In the past, a lot of people were worried about learning a coding language. They worried that these languages were too tough to learn, that they would just get frustrated, and that only those who had spent their whole lives around computers could even attempt to write their codes. And maybe with some of the older codes, this was true. Thanks to a lot of the newer codes that have been introduced recently, the idea that only those gifted in computer programming could code has faded away. With many of the codes that are coming out now, including Python, anyone can learn a few of the syntaxes for what they want to do, or even find some premade codes online and make some changes. And since many of these codes are open-sourced, it is easier than ever to learn how to use them and develop the codes to meet your needs. You will find that many of the modern languages that are used for coding are going to be a lot better and easier to use than what we were able to find in the past with most coding languages. Gone are the days that even professionals would run into troubles regularly when it was time to find the bugs in the system. Now anyone and everyone can learn how to use this coding language for these needs. And this is mainly because we have a lot of great OOP languages to work within Python.

Difference between Python 2 vs Python 3

There are many coding languages out there that you can use. Some of them are pretty basic to learn, and some have a bit more power behind them. Many people have at least interacted with Java or JavaScript when they go to a website, especially one that has a pop-up of any kind. If you have worked with a Windows computer, you may have experimented with some of the languages that are found there. Or maybe you are coming to this guidebook as a completely new beginner to all things coding and you want to know where to start.

The options can seem pretty overwhelming when you start. All the many languages are going to follow their own rules on how to write the codes and what you can do with the code as well. But if you are looking for a coding language that has a ton of power for a beginner, one that can easily stop and avoid others, one that offers you many choices and allows you to implement it with many other coding languages at the same time, then Python is the right choice for you.

Beginners and more advanced coders alike love working with the Python coding language. There are many benefits, but the primary part is that it was developed with the beginner in mind. In the last few decades, there has been a push in much of the world of technology to start making it easier to get more people to come in and join the fun. They see that there are benefits to inviting more people. More games can be created, more bugs fixed in programs, and just more innovation compared to the times when only a few people even had any idea how to code in the first place.

In this guidebook, we are going to spend some time exploring the world of Python, looking at what this coding language is all about, and helping you to write some of your codes by the time that you are done. Don't be scared about this coding language. While there are a lot of people who may be intimidated when they hear about coding because they worry it will be too hard, you will quickly see a ton of examples of how Python works. Then you will be ready to dive right in and see what your creativity and hard work can do.

CHAPTER 2:

ADVANTAGES AND DISADVANTAGES

Advantages of python language

It is Easy to Work with

The first benefit that most people are going to enjoy when it comes to using the Python language is that it is very easy to use. This language was designed for use with a beginner, and the whole purpose is to make sure that anyone, even those who may not be well-versed in doing any kind of programming at all, will be able to learn and write some of the codes of their own that they would like. This language is meant to help a beginner, someone who has never had a chance to work with coding in the past, learn how to do some of this coding, and get the results that they would like. There are also a lot of different things that you can do when you work with the Python coding language. It is designed to help with almost any kind of coding that you are interested in handling, from some of the basics of writing your projects to help out with data analysis and machine learning if you so choose. There is just so much that you can do with this kind of language and many people are jumping on board to learn how to work all of these different angles with ease thanks to the Python coding language.

It Has Lots of Power

Even though this is a coding language that is meant to help us out with some of the basics of coding, you will find that there is quite a bit of strength and power behind what we can do with it. Even more advanced problems can be easily handled when we are looking at this kind of language, and you will find that with the added extensions and libraries that are available with Python, it is easy to figure out how to write codes that work with some complex coding and programming problems Some people hear about how easy it is to work with Python and they worry that there is not going to be enough strength and power behind it to get started. They think they need to go with another option because this one will not have the strength of the features that are needed to get things done. But, once you mess around with some of the codes that we will do with this language, you will find that it is going to have plenty of power and a ton of the features that you need to get anything done.

21

Many Libraries to Work With

While we are at it, you will find that a lot of the libraries and extensions that come with the Python language are going to be great as well. You can already do a lot of work with the standard Python language, but you will also find that there are additional libraries that work well with Python and can help us to expand out what we can do with programming in this language. From libraries that can help us out with math, science, machine learning, data science, and more, you will find that the Python coding language is one of the best options for you to work with. From here, we will also find that the Python language is going to be one that can work well with others. For some of the basics that we will discuss in this guidebook, this is not going to seem like that big of a deal. But when we get into some things like machine learning and data science with this language, the fact that we can combine Python with other languages is going to help us get more done.

Easy to Read

We will also see that the Python coding language is going to be a great option to work with when you want to make sure that things stay organized and easy to read through. There are a lot of other coding languages out there that you can choose from, but that does not mean that they are the right ones for you. In most cases, beginners are going to find that working with an OOP language, just like Python is, is one of the best ways to keep the information organized and easy to use.

It is an OOP Language

The fact that Python is an OOP language is going to be good news for you. We will explore this a bit more in the next few chapters, but this basically means that the code is split up into classes, and then the objects that show up in the code will fit into one of these classes. This is the best way to make the code as efficient as possible and will ensure that you can bring up the right parts, at the right times so that your code will work the way that you want.

Disadvantages of Python language

Since it is an interpreted language it has been observed that it is often slower in execution than other languages.

Python is not compatible with many browsers and mobile computing.

Since the typing is dynamic therefore it requires more testing as the errors show up only during run time.

Now that we know about the pros and cons of Python, let us see in comparison with a few popular languages as to how Python stands out amongst them.

Python has been often compared to languages such as JavaScript, Java, Perl, Smalltalk, Tcl, and C++. These comparisons can be enlightening to know the nuances of this language. However, in a practical environment, the choice of a programming language is typically dictated by terms such as availability, training, prior investment, and of course the cost involved. Let us look at some comparisons which we have drawn with other languages:

Java—The programs run under Python are 3-5 times shorter than Java programs. This is due to the high level and dynamic typing of the language. The syntactic support is built directly into the language. For example, if you want to print "hello world" in Python one simply has to type: ***print ('hello world')*** whereas in Java the same command would be covered in 4 lines. Java Script-Unlike JavaScript, Python supports the writing of large programs with better codes by using object-oriented programming *Perl*- Both languages have a different philosophy where Perl supports common application-oriented tasks such as report generation, file scanning, etc., whereas Python supports common programming methods such as designing a data structure. It encourages programmers to write readable and maintainable codes.

Tcl—As compared to Python, Tcl is weak on data structures and executes codes which are much slower. It also lacks the feature of writing large scale programs.

Smalltalk—The standard library of Smalltalk is more defined whereas in the case of Python it has more facilities for dealing with the World Wide Web realities such as email, FTP, and HTML.

C++- Just like Java when compared to C++ the programming code is 5-10 times shorter. It is said that a C++ programmer can finish in a year Python programmer can finish in two months.

CHAPTER 3:

PYTHON INSTALLATION

Install Python on Linux

There are two ways to install Python on a Linux system – source installation or package-managed installation. While the latter is preferable, we will discuss both methods:

Package-Managed Installation

The most common method of installing Python on Linux is to use the Linux package systems. This also ensures that you can easily upgrade Python when the time comes. Depending on which distribution of Linux you are using, you will need to use one of these commands:

26

Debian-based, like Ubuntu

apt-get install python

RPM-based, like Red Hat or Fedora:

urpmi python

Gentoo:

emerge python

If you don't see the latest version of the installation, you will need to manually install Python, which we will talk about shortly.

You will need to install some extra packages if you want a full installation – these are optional but recommended if you want to be able to profile your programs or have code C extensions. To make sure you have a full installation, install these packages by typing them in at the command prompt:

- *python-dev* – has Python headers for use in compiling C modules

- *python-profiler* – has non-GPL modules for use on Debian, Ubuntu, and other full GPL Linux distributions

- *gcc* – used for compiling extensions that have C code in them

Compiling Sources

To do a manual installation, you need to use the cmmi process:

- Configure

- Make

- Make Install

This process will perform a Python compilation and then install it on your system.

To get the latest archive for Python, go to http://python.org.download

To perform the download, we use wget with MacPorts or apt – see www.gnu.org/software/wget for more information on your specific distribution.

To build Python, we are going to use gcc and make. Make is a program we use to read Makefile configuration files and make sure that all of the requirements are met to compile Python. It is also used as a way of driving the installation and it is invoked using the make and configure commands. gcc is better known as the GNU C Compiler and it is an open-source compiler that is used a lot in building programs. Ensure that both of these have been installed on your Linux system.

To build Python and install it, type in this command at the command prompt:

cd /tmp

wget http://python.org/ftp/python/2.5.1/Python2.5.1.tgz

tar -xzvf tar -xzvf Python2.5.1.tgz

cd Python2.5.1

./configure

make

sudo make install

This also installs all the headers for binary installations that are normally found in python-dev. Once all of this is installed, you should be able to reach Python from the Linux shell.

Install Python on Windows

We can install Python on a Windows system in the same way as a Linux, but this is an incredibly painful way of doing it. Instead, go to http://python.org/downlaod and download the version of Python that you want. All the instructions are provided, making it simple to do. Provided you do not change any of the defaults, you will find Python installed at c:\Python25 and not in the Program Files folder where you would expect to find it. This cuts out the risk of space in the path. Finally, we need to change the PATH environment variable, enabling us to get Python from the DOS shell. To do this:

- Find the icon for My Computer on your version of Windows and right-click on it

- This will open the System Properties dialog box

- Click on the tab for Advanced

- Click on the button for Environment Variables

Edit the PATH system variable to input two new paths, each separated with a semicolon (;). The paths to be added are:

- c:\Python25 – this will enable python.exe to be called

- c:\Python25\Scripts – this will enable installed third scripts to be called Python should now run in the command prompt. To open this, open the Run dialog box, press the Windows key and R at the same time. Type cmd in the box and click on Open. At the prompt type in *c:/>python* If you see a message like the one below, Python is installed:

Python 2.5.2 (#71, Oct 18 2006, 08:34:43) [MSC v.1310 32 bit (Intel)] on

win32

Type "help", "copyright", "credits" or "license" for more information.

\>>>

Python is ready to use.

Install Python on Mac

Although the Mac already comes with Python installed, this is likely to be out of date and is only good for learning, not for developing. The best thing is to install a new version of Python and to do that, we need a C compiler.

Go to the Mac App Store and download XCode

Open a terminal and type in xcode-select –install – this will install the command line tools

The next step is a package manager and the best one is called Homebrew and to install this, open a terminal and run the following code:

$ usrbin/ruby -e "$(curl -fsSL

https://raw.githubusercontent.com/Homebrew/install /master/install)"

Follow the on-screen instructions to install Homebrew and then prepare to make changes to the PATH environment variable. To do this, add this line at the bottom of the ~/.profile file: *export PATH=usrlocal/bin:usrlocal/sbin:$PATH*

Now you can install Python. For Python 2.7, type this is at the command:

$ brew install python

For Python 3, type this:

$ brew install python3

This will only take a couple of minutes at the most.

Homebrew will also install Pip and Setuptools. Setuptools lets you download and install Python software via a network, normally the Internet, using just a single command – *easy_install*. This will also let you add this capability for network installation to your Python software. Pip is used for the easy installation and management of Python packages and is recommended instead of using *easy_install*.

CHAPTER 4:

LEARNING PYTHON FROM SCRATCH

Data Types

Numbers

Python accommodates floating, integer, and complex numbers. The presence or absence of a decimal point separates integers and floating points. For instance, 4 is an integer while 4.0 is a floating-point number.

On the other hand, complex numbers in Python are denoted as r+tj where j represents the real part and t is the virtual part. In this context, the function type() is used to determine the variable class. The Python function is an instance() invoked to decide which specific class function originates from.

Example

Start IDLE.

Navigate to the File menu and click New Window.

Type the following:

number=6

 print(type(number)) #should output class int print(type(6.0)) #should output class float complex_num=7+5j

print(complex_num+5)

print(isinstance(complex_num, complex)) #should output True Important: Integers in Python can be of infinite length. Floating numbers in Python are assumed precise up to fifteen decimal places.

Number Conversion

This segment assumes you have prior basic knowledge of how to manually or using a calculator to convert decimal into binary, octal, and hexadecimal.

Check out the Windows Calculator in Windows 10, Calculator version 10.1804.911.1000 and choose programmer mode to automatically convert.

Programmers often need to convert decimal numbers into octal, hexadecimal, and binary forms. A prefix in Python allows the denotation of these numbers to their corresponding type.

Number System Prefix

Octal '0O' or '0o'

Binary '0B' or '0b'

Hexadecimal '0X or '0x'

Example

print(0b1010101) #Output:85

print(0x7B+0b0101)   #Output: 128   (123+5)   print(0o710) #Output:710

Assignment

Create a program in Python to display the following: i) 0011 11112

ii) 7478

iii) 9316

Type Conversion

Sometimes referred to as coercion, type conversion allows us to change one type of number into another. The preloaded functions such as float(), int() and complex() enable implicit and explicit type conversions.

The same functions can be used to change from strings.

Example

Start IDLE.

Navigate to the File menu and click New Window.

Type the following:

int(5.3) #Gives 5

int(5.9) #Gives 5

The int() will produce a truncation effect when applied to float numbers. It will simply drop the decimal point part without rounding off. For the float() let us take a look: Start IDLE.

Navigate to the File menu and click New Window.

Type the following:

float(6) #Gives 6.0

complex('4+2j') #Gives (4+2j)

Assignment

Apply the int() conversion to the following: a. 4.1

b. 4.7

c. 13.3

d. 13.9

Apply the float() conversion to the following: e. 7

f. 16

g. 19

Decimal in Python

Example

Start IDLE.

Navigate to the File menu and click New Window.

Type the following:

(1.2+2.1)==3.3 #Will return False, why?

Explanation The computer works with finite numbers and fractions cannot be stored in their raw form as they will create an infinitely long binary sequence.

Fractions in Python

The fractions module in Python allows operations on fractional numbers.

Example

Start IDLE.

Navigate to the File menu and click New Window.

Type the following:

Important

Creating my_fraction from float can lead to unusual results due to the misleading representation of binary floating-point.

Mathematics in Python

To carry out mathematical functions, Python offers modules like random and math.

Start IDLE.

Navigate to the File menu and click New Window.

Type the following:

```
import math

print(math.pi) #output:3.14159....

print(math.cos(math.pi)) #the output will be -1.0

print(math.exp(10)) #the output will be 22026.4....

print(math.log10(100)) #the output will be 2

print(math.factorial(5)) #the output will be 120
```

Exercise

Write a python program that uses math functions from the math module to perform the following: a. Square of 34

b. Log1010000

c. Cos 45 x sin 90

d. Exponent of 20

Lists in Python

We create a list in Python by placing items called elements inside square brackets separated by commas. The items in a list can be of a mixed data type.

Start IDLE.

Navigate to the File menu and click New Window.

Type the following:

list_mine=[] #empty list list_mine=[2,5,8] #list of integers list_mine=[5,"Happy", 5.2] #list having mixed data types

Assignment

Write a program that captures the following in a list: "Best", 26,89,3.9

Nested Lists

A nested list is a list as an item in another list.

Example

Start IDLE.

Navigate to the File menu and click New Window.

Type the following:

list_mine=["carrot", [9, 3, 6], ['g']]

Exercise

Write a nested for the following elements: [36,2,1],"Writer",'t',[3.0, 2.5]

Accessing Elements from a List

In programming and Python specifically, the first time is always indexed zero. For a list of five items, we will access them from index0 to index4. Failure to access the items in a list in this manner will create an index error. The index is always an integer as using other number types will create a type error. For nested lists, they are accessed via nested indexing.

Example

Start IDLE.

Navigate to the File menu and click New Window.

Type the following:

list_mine=['b','e','s','t']

print(list_mine[0]) #the output will be b print(list_mine[2]) #the output will be s print(list_mine[3]) #the output will be t *Exercise*

Given the following list:

your_collection=['t','k','v','w','z','n','f']

a. Create a program in Python to display the second item in the list b. Create a program in Python to display the sixth item in the last c. Create a program in Python to display the last item in the list.

Nested List Indexing
Start IDLE.

Navigate to the File menu and click New Window.

Type the following:

nested_list=["Best",[4,7,2,9]]

print(nested_list[0][1]

Python Negative Indexing
For its sequences, Python allows negative indexing. The last item on the list is index-1, index -2 is the second last item, and so on.

Start IDLE.

Navigate to the File menu and click New Window.

Type the following:

list_mine=['c','h','a','n','g','e','s']

print(list_mine[-1]) #Output is s print(list_mine [-4]) ##Output is n Slicing Lists in Python

Slicing operator (full colon) is used to access a range of elements in a list.

Example

Start IDLE.

Navigate to the File menu and click New Window.

Type the following:

list_mine=['c','h','a','n','g','e','s']

print(list_mine[3:5]) #Picking elements from the 4 to the sixth
Example

Picking elements from start to the fifth Start IDLE.

Navigate to the File menu and click New Window.

Type the following:

print(list_mine[:-6])

Example

Picking the third element to the last.

print(list_mine[2:])

Exercise

Given class_names=['John', 'Kelly', 'Yvonne', 'Una','Lovy','Pius', 'Tracy']

a. Write a python program using a slice operator to display from the second students and the rest.

b. Write a python program using a slice operator to display the first student to the third using a negative indexing feature.

c. Write a python program using a slice operator to display the fourth and fifth students only.

Manipulating Elements in a List using the assignment operator

Items in a list can be changed meaning lists are mutable.

Start IDLE.

Navigate to the File menu and click New Window.

Type the following:

list_yours=[4,8,5,2,1]

list_yours[1]=6

print(list_yours) #The output will be [4,6,5,2,1]

Changing a range of items in a list

Start IDLE.

Navigate to the File menu and click New Window.

Type the following:

list_yours[0:3]=[12,11,10] #Will change first item to fourth item in the list print(list_yours) #Output will be: [12,11,10,1]

Appending/Extending items in the List

The append() method allows extending the items in the list. The extend() can also be used.

Example

Start IDLE.

Navigate to the File menu and click New Window.

Type the following:

list_yours=[4, 6, 5]

list_yours.append(3)

print(list_yours) #The output will be [4,6,5, 3]

Example

Start IDLE.

Navigate to the File menu and click New Window.

Type the following:

list_yours=[4,6,5]

list_yours.extend([13,7,9]) print(list_yours) #The output will be [4,6,5,13,7,9]

The plus operator(+) can also be used to combine two lists. The * operator can be used to perform an iteration of a list of given several.

Example

Start IDLE.

Navigate to the File menu and click New Window.

Type the following:

list_yours=[4,6,5]

print(list_yours+[13,7,9]) # Output:[4, 6, 5,13,7,9]

print(['happy']*4) #Output:["happy","happy", "happy","happy"]

Removing or Deleting Items from a List

The keyword del is used to delete elements or the entire list in Python.

Example

Start IDLE.

Navigate to the File menu and click New Window.

Type the following:

list_mine=['t','r','o','g','r','a','m']

del list_mine[1]

print(list_mine) #t, o, g, r, a, m

Deleting Multiple Elements

Example

Start IDLE.

Navigate to the File menu and click New Window.

Type the following:

del list_mine[0:3]

Example

print(list_mine) #a, m

Delete Entire List

Start IDLE.

Navigate to the File menu and click New Window.

Type the following:

delete list_mine

print(list_mine) #will generate an error of lost not found The remove() method or pop() function may be used to remove the specified item. The pop() method will remove and return the last item if the index is not given and helps implement lists as stacks. The clear() method is used to empty a list.

Start IDLE.

Navigate to the File menu and click New Window.

Type the following:

list_mine=['t','k','b','d','w','q','v']

list_mine.remove('t')

print(list_mine) #output will be ['t','k','b','d','w','q','v']

print(list_mine.pop(1)) #output will be 'k'

print(list_mine.pop()) #output will be 'v'

Assignment

Given list_yours=['K','N','O','C','K','E','D']

a. Pop the third item in the list, save the program as list1.

b. Remove the fourth item using remove() method and save the program as list2

c. Delete the second item in the list and save the program as list3.

d. Pop the list without specifying an index and save the program as list4.

Using Empty List to Delete an entire or specific element

Start IDLE.

Navigate to the File menu and click New Window.

Type the following:

list_mine=['t','k','b','d','w','q','v']

list_mine=[1:2]=[]

print(list_mine) #Output will be ['t','w','q','v']

List Methods in Python

Assignment

Use list access methods to display the following items in reversed order list_yours=[4,9,2,1,6,7]

Use list access method to count the elements in a.

Use the list access method to sort the items in a. in an ascending order/default.

Inbuilt Python Functions that can be used to manipulate Python Lists

In Python, lists are collections of data types that can be changed, organized, and include duplicate values. Lists are written within square brackets, as shown in the syntax below.

X = ["string001", "string002", "string003"]

print (X)

The same concept of position applies to Lists as the string data type, which dictates that the first string is considered to be at position 0. Subsequently, the strings that will follow are given positions 1, 2, and so on. You can selectively display the desired string from a List by referencing the position of that string inside the square bracket in the print command, as shown below.

X = ["string001", "string002", "string003"]

print (X [2])

OUTPUT – [string003]

Similarly, the concept of *negative indexing* is also applied to Python List. Let's look at the example below:

X = ["string001", "string002", "string003"]

print (X [-2])

OUTPUT – [string002]

You will also be able to specify a *range of indexes* by indicating the start and end of a range. The result in values of such command on a Python List would be a new List containing only the indicated items. Here is an example for your reference.

X = ["string001", "string002", "string003", "string004", "string005", "string006"]

print (X [2 : 4])

OUTPUT – ["string003", "string004"]

* Remember the first item is at position 0, and the final position of the range (4) is not included.

Now, if you do not indicate the start of this range, it will default to the position 0 as shown in the example below:

X = ["string001", "string002", "string003", "string004", "string005", "string006"]

print (X [: 3])

OUTPUT – ["string001", "string002", "string003"]

Similarly, if you do not indicate the end of this range it will display all the items of the List from the indicated start range to the end of the List, as shown in the example below:

X = ["string001", "string002", "string003", "string004", "string005", "string006"] print (X [3 :])

OUTPUT – ["string004", "string005", "string006"]

You can also specify a *range of negative indexes* to Python Lists, as shown in the example below: X = ["string001", "string002", "string003", "string004", "string005", "string006"]

print (X [-3 : -1])

OUTPUT – ["string004", "string005"]

* Remember the last item is at position -1, and the final position of this range (-1) is not included in the Output.

There might be instances when you need to *change the data value* for a Python List. This can be accomplished by referring to the index number of that item and declaring the new value. Let's look at the example below: X = ["string001", "string002", "string003", "string004", "string005", "string006"]

X [3] = "newstring"

print (X)

OUTPUT – ["string001", "string002", "string003", "newstring", "string005", "string006"]

You can also determine the *length* of a Python List using the "len()" function, as shown in the example below: X = ["string001", "string002", "string003", "string004", "string005", "string006"] print (len (X))

OUTPUT – 6

Python Lists can also be changed by *adding new items* to an existing list using the built-in "append ()" method, as shown in the example below: X = ["string001", "string002", "string003", "string004"]

X.append ("newstring")

print (X)

OUTPUT – ["string001", "string002", "string003", "string004", "newstring"]

You can also, add a new item to an existing Python List at a specific position using the built-in "insert ()" method, as shown in the example below: X = ["string001", "string002", "string003", "string004"]

X.insert (2, "newstring")

print (X)

OUTPUT – ["string001", "string002", "newstring", "string004"]

there might be instances when you need to *copy* an existing Python List. This can be accomplished by using the built-in "copy ( )" method or the "list ( )" method, as shown in the example below: *X = ["string001", "string002", "string003", "string004", "string005", "string006"]*

Y = X.copy( )

print (Y)

OUTPUT – ["string001", "string002", "string003", "string004", "string005", "string006"]

X = ["string001", "string002", "string003", "string004", "string005", "string006"]

Y = list (X)

print (Y)

OUTPUT – ["string001", "string002", "string003", "string004", "string005", "string006"]

There are multiple built-in methods to *delete items* from a Python List.

• To selectively delete a specific item, the "remove ()" method can be used.

X = ["string001", "string002", "string003", "string004"]

X.remove ("string002")

print (X)

OUTPUT - ["string001", "string003", "string004"]

- To delete a specific item from the List, the "pop ()" method can be used with the position of the value. If no index has been indicated, the last item of the index will be removed.

X = ["string001", "string002", "string003", "string004"]

X.pop ( )

print (X)

OUTPUT - ["string001", "string002", "string003"]

- To delete a specific index from the List, the "del ()" method can be used, followed by the index within square brackets.

X = ["string001", "string002", "string003", "string004"]

del X [2]

print (X)

OUTPUT - ["string001", "string002", "string004"]

- To delete the entire List variable, the "del ()" method can be used, as shown below.

X = ["string001", "string002", "string003", "string004"]

del X

OUTPUT - .....

- To delete all the string values from the List without deleting the variable itself, the "clear ()" method can be used, as shown below.

X = ["string001", "string002", "string003", "string004"]

X.clear()

print (X)

OUTPUT – [ ]

Concatenation of Lists

You can join multiple lists with the use of the "+" logical operator or by adding all the items from one list to another using the "append ( )" method. The "extend ( )" method can be used to add a list at the end of another list. Let's look at the examples below to understand these commands.

X = ["string001", "string002", "string003", "string004"]

Y = [10, 20, 30, 40]

Z = X + Y

print (Z)

OUTPUT – ["string001", "string002", "string003", "string004", 10, 20, 30, 40]

X = ["string001", "string002", "string003", "string004"]

Y = [10, 20, 30, 40]

For x in Y:

X.append (x)

print (X)

OUTPUT – ["string001", "string002", "string003", "string004", 10, 20, 30, 40]

X = ["string001", "string002", "string003"]

Y = [10, 20, 30]

X.extend (Y)

print (X)

OUTPUT – ["string001", "string002", "string003", 10, 20, 30]

Exercise

Create a list "A" with string data values as "red, olive, cyan, lilac, mustard" and display the item at -2 position.

Use Your Discretion Here And Write Your Code First

Now, check your code against the correct code below:

A = ["red", "olive", "cyan", "lilac", "mustard"]

print (A [-2])

OUTPUT – ["lilac"]

Exercise

Create a list "A" with string data values as "red, olive, cyan, lilac, mustard" and display the items ranging from the string on the second position to the end of the string.

Use Your Discretion Here And Write Your Code First

Now, check your code against the correct code below:

A = ["red", "olive", "cyan", "lilac", "mustard"]

print (A [2 :])

OUTPUT – ["cyan", "lilac", "mustard"]

Exercise

Create a list "A" with string data values as "red, olive, cyan, lilac, mustard" and replace the string "olive" to "teal".

Use Your Discretion Here And Write Your Code First

Now, check your code against the correct code below:

A = ["red", "olive", "cyan", "lilac", "mustard"]

A [1] = ["teal"]

print (A)

OUTPUT – ["red", "teal", "cyan", "lilac", "mustard"]

Exercise

Create a list "A" with string data values as "red, olive, cyan, lilac, mustard" and copy the list "A" to create a list "B".

Use Your Discretion Here And Write Your Code First

Now, check your code against the correct code below:

A = ["red", "olive", "cyan", "lilac", "mustard"]

B = A.copy ( )

print (B)

OUTPUT – ["red", "olive", "cyan", "lilac", "mustard"]

Exercise

Create a list "A" with string data values as "red, olive, cyan, lilac, mustard" and delete the strings "red" and "lilac".

Use Your Discretion Here And Write Your Code First

Now, check your code against the correct code below:

A = ["red", "olive", "cyan", "lilac", "mustard"]

del.A [0, 2]

print (A)

OUTPUT – ["olive", "cyan", "mustard"]

String in Python

Python strings are competent to usually make use of single or double quotation marks, plus you're in a position to utilize quotation marks of only one type in a string using an additional kind, consequently, the following is valid:

This is a valid' string

Multi-strings are enclosed in specific or perhaps triple two-fold quotes. Python can support Unicode immediately, using the following syntax:

Flow management statements Python's flow management statements are while', for' and if'. For a switch, you've to use if'. For enumerating by show participants, use for'. For getting a choice checklist, use range (amount). Here is the declaration syntax: range list = range(10)

>>>; print range list

[0, 8, 7, 6, 5, 4, 3, 2, 1, 9]

for quantity in range list:

if the number in (three, 7, 4, 9):

break

else:

continue

```
else:

pass

if perhaps rangelist[1] == 2:

print The next item (lists are 0 based) is 2

Elif rangelist[1] == 3:

print The next item (lists are 0 based) is 3

else:

print documents Dunno

while rangelist[1] == 1:

pass
```

Example

Start IDLE.

Navigate to the File menu and click New Window.

Type the following:

```
string_mine = 'Colorful'

print(string_mine)

string_mine = "Hello"
```

```
print(string_mine)

string_mine = '"Hello"'

print(string_mine)

string_mine = """"I feel like I have been born a programmer"""

print(string_mine)
```

Accessing items in a string

Example

Start IDLE.

Navigate to the File menu and click New Window.

Type the following:

```
str = 'Colorful'

print('str = ', str)

print('str[1] = ', str[1]) #Output the second item print('str[-2] = ', str[-2]) #Output the second last item print('str[2:4] = ', str[2:4]) #Output the third through the fifth item
```

Deleting or Changing in Python

In Python, strings are immutable therefore cannot be changed once assigned. However, deleting the entire string is possible.

Example

Start IDLE.

Navigate to the File menu and click New Window.

Type the following:

del string_mine

String Operations

Several operations can be performed on a string making it a widely used data type in Python.

Concatenation using the + operator, repetition using the * operator Example

Start IDLE.

Navigate to the File menu and click New Window.

Type the following:

string1='Welcome'

string2='Again'

print('string1+string2=',string1+string2) print(' string1 * 3 =', string1 * 3) Exercise

Given string_a=" I am awake" and string_b="coding in Python in a pajama"

String Iteration

The for-control statement is used to continually scan through an entire scan until the specified several are reached before terminating the scan.

Example

Start IDLE.

Navigate to the File menu and click New Window.

Type the following:

Membership Test in String

The keyword is used to test if a substring exists.

Example

't' in "triumph' #Will return True Inbuilt Python Functions for working with Strings They include enumerate () and len().The len() function returns the length of the string.

String Formatting in Python

Escape Sequences Single and Double Quotes

Example

Start IDLE.

Navigate to the File menu and click New Window.

Type the following:

print('They said, "We need a new team?"') # escape with single quotes
escaping double quotes

print("They said, \" We need a new team\"")

Escape Sequences in Python

The escape sequences enable us to format our output to enhance clarity to the human user.

A program will still run successfully without using escape sequences but the output will be highly confusing to the human user.

Writing and displaying output in expected output is part of good programming practices.

The following are commonly used escape sequences.

Examples

Start IDLE.

65

Navigate to the File menu and click New Window.

Type the following:

print("D:\\Lessons\\Programming") print("Prints\n in two lines")

Working with Files

Programs are made with input and output in mind.

You input data to the program, the program processes the input, and it ultimately provides you with output.

For example, a calculator will take in numbers and operations you want.

It will then process the operation you wanted.

And then, it will display the result to you as its output.

There are multiple ways for a program to receive input and to produce output.

One of those ways is to read and write data on files.

To start learning how to work with files, you need to learn the open() function.

The open() function has one *required* parameter and two *optional* parameters.

The first and required parameter is the file name.

The second parameter is the access mode. And the third parameter is buffering or buffer size.

The filename parameter requires string data.

The access mode requires string data, but there is a set of string values that you can use and is defaulted to "r".

The buffer size parameter requires an integer and is defaulted to 0.

To practice using the open() function, create a file with the name sampleFile.txt inside your Python directory.

Try this sample code:

```
>>> file1 = open("sampleFile.txt")

>>> _
```

Note that the file function returns a file object.

The statement in the example assigns the file object to variable file1.

The file object has multiple attributes, and three of them are:

name: This contains the name of the file.

mode: This contains the access mode you used to access the file.

closed: This returns False if the file has been opened and True if the file is closed. When you use the open() function, the file is set to open.

Now, access those attributes.

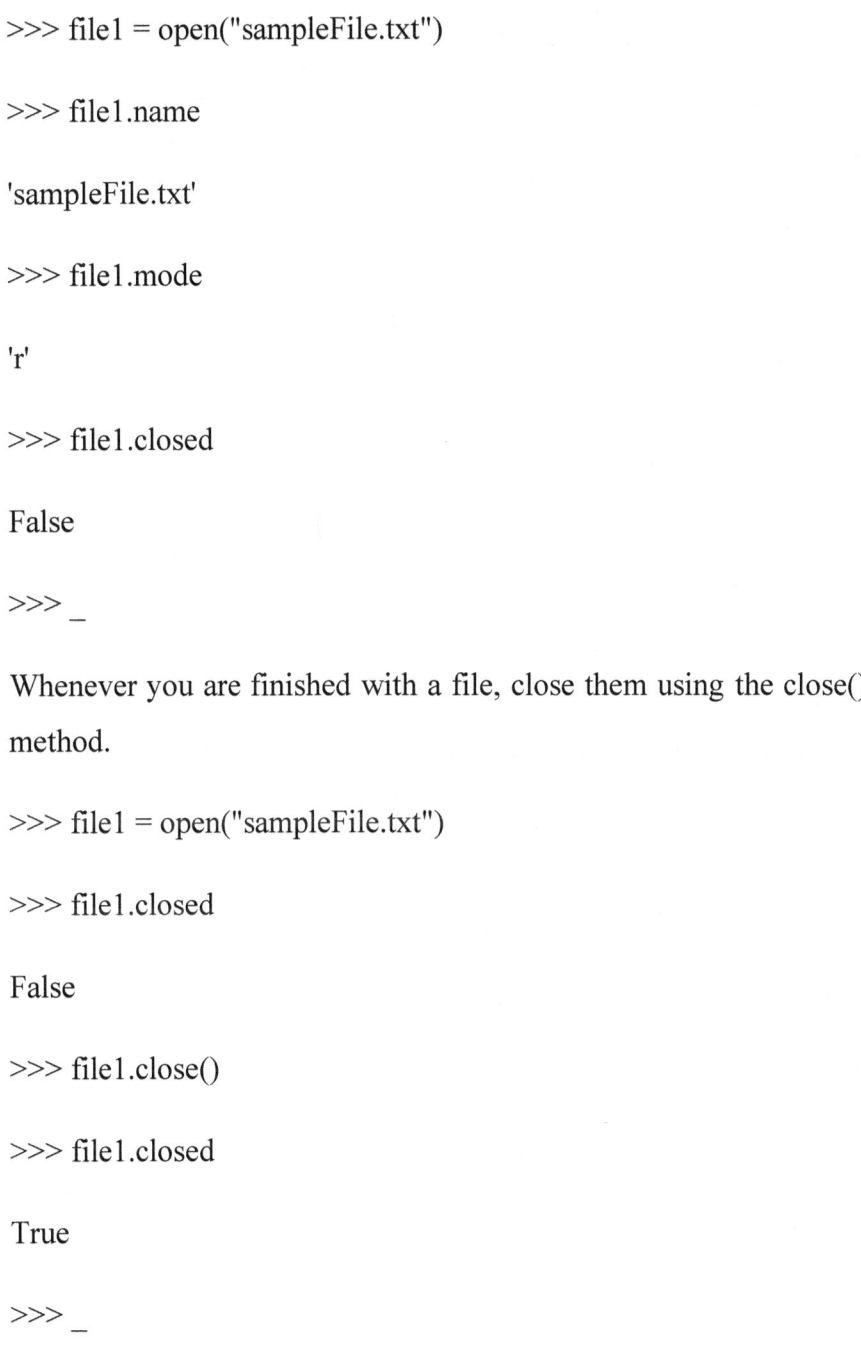

```
>>> file1 = open("sampleFile.txt")

>>> file1.name

'sampleFile.txt'

>>> file1.mode

'r'

>>> file1.closed

False

>>> _
```

Whenever you are finished with a file, close them using the close() method.

```
>>> file1 = open("sampleFile.txt")

>>> file1.closed

False

>>> file1.close()

>>> file1.closed

True

>>> _
```

Remember that closing the file does not delete the variable or object.

To reopen the file, just open and reassign the file object.

For example:

```
>>> file1 = open("sampleFile.txt")

>>> file1.close()

>>> file1 = open(file1.name)

>>> file1.closed

False

>>> _
```

Reading from a File

Before proceeding, open the sampleFile.txt in your text editor.

Type "Hello World" in it and save.

Go back to Python.

To read the contents of the file, use the read() method.

For example:

```
>>> file1 = open("sampleFile.txt")

>>> file1.read()

'Hello World'

>>> _
```

69

File Pointer

Whenever you access a file, Python sets the file pointer.

The file pointer is like your word processor's cursor.

Any operation on the file starts at where the file pointer is.

When you open a file, and when it is set to the default access mode, which is "r" (read-only), the file pointer is set at the beginning of the file.

To know the current position of the file pointer, you can use the tell() method.

For example:

```
>>> file1 = open("sampleFile.txt")
>>> file1.tell()
0
>>> 
```

Most of the actions you perform on the file move the file pointer.

For example:

```
>>> file1 = open("sampleFile.txt")
>>> file1.tell()
0
```

```
>>> file1.read()

'Hello World'

>>> file1.tell()

11

>>> file1.read()

''

>>> _
```

To move the file pointer to a position you desire, you can use the seek() function.

For example:

```
>>> file1 = open("sampleFile.txt")

>>> file1.tell()

0

>>> file1.read()

'Hello World'

>>> file1.tell()

11

>>> file1.seek(0)
```

0

>>> file1.read()

'Hello World'

>>> file1.seek(1)

1

>>> file1.read()

'ello World'

>>> _

The seek() method has two parameters.

The first is offset, which sets the pointer's position depending on the second parameter.

Also, an argument for this parameter is required.

The second parameter is optional.

It is for whence, which dictates where the "seek" will start.

It is set to 0 by default.

If set to 0, Python will set the pointer's position to the offset argument.

If set to 1, Python will set the pointer's position relative or in addition to the current position of the pointer.

If set to 2, Python will set the pointer's position relative or in addition to the file's end.

Note that the last two options require the access mode to have binary access. If the access mode does not have binary access, the last two options will be useful to determine the current position of the pointer [seek(0, 1)] and the position at the end of the file [seek(0, 2)].

For example:

```
>>> file1 = open("sampleFile.txt")

>>> file1.tell()

0

>>> file1.seek(1)

1

>>> file1.seek(0, 1)

0

>>> file1.seek(0, 2)

11

>>> _
```

File Access Modes

To write to a file, you will need to know more about file access modes in Python.

There are three types of file operations: reading, writing and appending.

Reading allows you to access and copy any part of the file's content.

Writing allows you to overwrite a file's contents and create a new one.

Appending allows you to write on the file while keeping the other content intact.

There are two types of file access modes: string and binary.

String access allows you to access a file's content as if you are opening a text file.

Binary access allows you to access a file on its rawest form: binary.

In your sample file, accessing it using string access allows you to read the line "Hello World".

Accessing the file using binary access will let you read "Hello World" in binary, which will be b'Hello World'.

For example:

```
>>> x = open("sampleFile.txt", "rb")
```

```
>>> x.read()

b'Hello World'

>>> _
```

String access is useful for editing text files.

Binary access is useful for anything else, like pictures, compressed files, and executables. In this book, you will only be taught how to handle text files.

There are multiple values that you can enter in the file access mode parameter of the open() function.

But you do not need to memorize the combination.

You just need to know the letter combinations.

Each letter and symbol stand for an access mode and operation.

For example:

r = read-only—file pointer placed at the beginning

r+ = read and write

a = append—file pointer placed at the end

a+ = read and append

w = overwrite/create—file pointer set to 0 since you create the file w+ = read and overwrite/create

b = binary

By default, file access mode is set to string.

You need to add b to allow binary access.

For example "rb".

Writing to a File

When writing to a file, you must always remember that Python overwrites and does not insert files.

For example:

```
>>> x = open("sampleFile.txt", "r+")
>>> x.read()
'Hello World'
>>> x.tell(0)
0
>>> x.write("text")
4
>>> x.tell()
4
```

>>> x.read()

'o World'

>>> x.seek(0)

0

>>> x.read()

'texto World'

>>> _

You might have expected that the resulting text will be "textHello World".

The write method of the file object replaces each character one by one, starting from the current position of the pointer.

Practice Exercise

For practice, you need to perform the following tasks:

Create a new file named test.txt.

Write the entire practice exercise instructions on the file.

Close the file and reopen it.

Read the file and set the cursor back to 0.

Close the file and open it using append access mode.

Add a rewritten version of these instructions at the end of the file.

Create a new file and put similar content to it by copying the contents of the test.txt file.

Working with files in Python is easy to understand but difficult to implement.

As you already saw, there are only a few things that you need to remember.

The hard part is when you are accessing the file.

Remember that the key things that you should master are the access modes and the management of the file pointer.

It is easy to get lost in a file that contains a thousand characters.

Aside from being versed in the file operations, you should also supplement your learning with the functions and methods of the str class in Python.

Most of the time, you will be dealing with strings if you need to work on a file.

Do not worry about binary yet.

That is a different beast altogether and you will only need to tame it when you are already adept at Python. As a beginner, expect that you will not deal yet with binary files that often contain media information.

Anyway, the next lesson is an elaboration on the "try" and "except" statements.

You'll discover how to manage and handle errors and exceptions effectively.

Python Tuples

In Python, Tuples are collections of data types that cannot be changed but can be arranged in a specific order. Tuples allow for duplicate items and are written within round brackets, as shown in the syntax below.

Tuple = ("string001", "string002", "string003")

print (Tuple)

Tuples are similar to lists and creating them is quite simple, one has to put commas to separate values and these values can also be enclosed in parenthesis. For example: *tup1* = *('chemistry', 'physics', 1998, 2000); tup2* = *(7, 8, 9); tup3* = *"x", "y", "z" ; Listed below are some of the basic features of tuple:*

a) For writing an empty tuple two parentheses are used – *tup1* = *();*

b) Even of the tuple contains a single value one has to include comma—*tup1* = *(50,);*

c) The indices in tuple start with at 0 and slicing can also be done.

d) Square brackets are used to access values in tuples

e) One cannot change or update the values in tuples

f) Removing the tuple element is not possible; however one can use *del* to remove the entire tuple.

g) All general operators can be used There are few built-in tuples like:

For comparing different elements - cmp(tuple1, tuple2)

To find the total length of tuple -len(tuple)

Converting a list to tuple – tuple(seq)

Find maximum value—max(tuple)

Minimum value – min(tuple)

Similar to the Python List, you can selectively display the desired string from a Tuple by referencing the position of that string inside the square bracket in the print command as shown below.

Tuple = ("string001", "string002", "string003")

print (Tuple [1])

OUTPUT – ("string002")

The concept of *negative indexing* can also be applied to Python Tuple, as shown in the example below: *Tuple = ("string001", "string002", "string003", "string004", "string005")*

print (Tuple [-2])

OUTPUT – ("string004")

You will also be able to specify a *range of indexes* by indicating the start and end of a range. The result in values of such command on a Python Tuple would be a new Tuple containing only the indicated items, as shown in the example below:

Tuple = ("string001", "string002", "string003", "string004", "string005", "string006")

print (Tuple [1:5])

Output

("string002", "string003", "string004", "string005")

* Remember the first item is at position 0 and the final position of the range, which is the fifth position in this example, is not included.

You can also specify a **range of negative indexes** *to Python Tuples, as shown in the example below:* Tuple = ("string001", "string002", "string003", "string004", "string005", "string006")

print (Tuple [-4: -2])

Output – ("string004", "string005")

* Remember the last item is at position -1 and the final position of this range, which is the negative fourth position in this example is not included in the Output.

Unlike Python lists, you cannot directly *change the data value of Python Tuples* after they have been created. However, conversion of a Tuple into a List and then modifying the data value of that List will allow you to subsequently create a Tuple from that updated List. Let's look at the example below: Tuple1 = *("string001", "string002", "string003", "string004", "string005", "string006") List1 = list (Tuple1)*

List1 [2] = "update this list to create new tuple"

Tuple1 = tuple (List1)

print (Tuple1)

Output – ("string001", "string002", "update this list to create new tuple", "string004", "string005", "string006")

You can also determine the *length* of a Python Tuple using the "len()" function, as shown in the example below: ***Tuple = ("string001", "string002", "string003", "string004", "string005", "string006")***

print (len (Tuple))

Output – *6*

You cannot selectively delete items from a Tuple, but you can use the "del" keyword to *delete the Tuple* in its entirety, as shown in the example below: *Tuple = ("string001", "string002", "string003", "string004")* del Tuple

print (Tuple)

Output – name 'Tuple' is not defined

You can *join multiple Tuples* with the use of the "+" logical operator.

Tuple1 = ("string001", "string002", "string003", "string004")

Tuple2 = (100, 200, 300)

Tuple3 = Tuple1 + Tuple2

print (Tuple3)

Output – ("string001", "string002", "string003", "string004", 100, 200, 300)

You can also use the "tuple ( )" constructor to create a Tuple, as shown in the example below:

Tuple1 = tuple (("string001", "string002", "string003", "string004"))

print (Tuple1)

Example

Start IDLE.

Navigate to the File menu and click New Window.

Type the following:

tuple_mine = (21, 12, 31)

print(tuple_mine)

tuple_mine = (31, "Green", 4.7) print(tuple_mine)

Accessing Python Tuple Elements *Example*

Start IDLE.

Navigate to the File menu and click New Window.

Type the following:

tuple_mine=['t','r','o','g','r','a','m']

print(tuple_mine[1]) #output:'r'

print(tuple_mine[3]) #output:'g'

Negative Indexing

Just like lists, tuples can also be indexed negatively.

Like lists, -1 refers to the last element on the list and -2 refers to the second last element.

Example

Start IDLE.

Navigate to the File menu and click New Window.

Type the following:

tuple_mine=['t','r','o','g','r','a','m']

print(tuple_mine [-2]) #the output will be 'a'

Slicing

The slicing operator, the full colon is used to access a range of items in a tuple.

Example

Start IDLE.

Navigate to the File menu and click New Window.

Type the following:

tuple_mine=['t','r','o','g','r','a','m']

print(tuple_mine [2:5]) #Output: 'o','g','r','a'

print(tuple_mine[:-4]) #'g','r','a','m'

Note

Tuple elements are immutable meaning they cannot be changed. However, we can combine elements in a tuple using +(concatenation operator). We can also repeat elements in a tuple using the * operator, just like lists.

Example

Start IDLE.

Navigate to the File menu and click New Window.

Type the following:

print((7, 45, 13) + (17, 25, 76)) print(("Several",) * 4) *Note*

Since we cannot change elements in a tuple, we cannot delete the elements too.

However, removing the full tuple can be attained using the keyword del.

Example

Start IDLE.

Navigate to the File menu and click New Window.

Type the following:

t_mine=['t','k','q','v','y','c','d']

del t_mine

Available Tuple Methods in Python

There are only two methods available for working Python tuples.

count(y)

When called will give the item numbers that are equal to y.

index(y)

When called will give the index first item index that is equal to y.

Example

Start IDLE.

Navigate to the File menu and click New Window.

Type the following:

t_mine=['t','k','q','v','y','c','d']

print(t_mine.count('t'))

print(t_mine.index('l'))

Testing Membership in Tuple

The keyword in us used to check the specified element exists in a tuple.

Start IDLE.

Navigate to the File menu and click New Window.

Type the following:

t_mine=['t','k','q','v','y','c','d']

print('a' t_mine) #Output: True print('k' in t_mine) #Output: False

Exercise

Create a Tuple "X" with string data values as "pies, cake, bread, scone, cookies" and display the item at -3 position.

Use Your Discretion Here And Write Your Code First

Now, check your code against the correct code below:

X = ("pies", "cake", "bread", "scone", "cookies")

print (X [-3])

Output – ("bread")

Exercise

Create a Tuple "X" with string data values as "pies, cake, bread, scone, cookies" and display items ranging from -2 to -4.

Use Your Discretion Here And Write Your Code First

Now, check your code against the correct code below:

X = ("pies", "cake", "bread", "scone", "cookies")

print (X [-4 : -2])

Output – ("cake", "bread")

Exercise

Create a Tuple "X" with string data values as "pies, cake, bread, scone, cookies" and change its item from "cookies" to "start" using the List function.

Use Your Discretion Here And Write Your Code First

Now, check your code against the correct code below:

X = ("pies", "cake", "bread", "scone", "cookies")

Y = list (X)

Y [4] = "tart"

X = tuple (Y)

print (X)

Output – ("pies", "cake", "bread", "scone", "tart")

Exercise

Create a Tuple "X" with string data values as "pies, cake, cookies" and another Tuple "Y" with numeric data values as (2, 12, 22), then join them together.

Use Your Discretion Here And Write Your Code First

Now, check your code against the correct code below:

X = ("pies", "cake", "cookies")

Y = (2, 12, 22)

Z = X + Y

print (Z)

Output – ("pies", "cake", "cookies", 2, 12, 22)

Python Sets

In Python, Sets are collections of data types that cannot be organized and indexed. Sets do not allow for duplicate items and must be written within curly brackets, as shown in the syntax below: *set = {"string1", "string2", "string3"}*

print (set)

Unlike the Python List and Tuple, you cannot selectively display desired items from a Set by referencing the position of that item because the Python Set is not arranged in any order. Therefore, items do not have any indexing. However, the "for" loop can be used on Sets (more on this topic later in this chapter).

Unlike Python Lists, you cannot directly *change the data values of Python Sets* after they have been created. However, you can use the "add ()" method to add a single item to Set and use the "update ( )" method to add one or more items to an already existing Set. Let's look at the example below: *set = {"string1", "string2", "string3"}*

set. add ("newstring")

print (set)

Output – {"string1", "string2", "string3", "newstring"}

set = {"string1", "string2", "string3"}

set. update (["newstring1", "newstring2", "newstring3",)

print (set)

Output – {"string1", "string2", "string3", "newstring1", "newstring2", "newstring3"}

You can also determine the *length* of a Python Set using the "len()" function, as shown in the example below: *set = {"string1", "string2", "string3", "string4", "string5", "string6", "string7"}*

print (len(set))

Output – 7

To selectively delete a specific item from a Set, the "remove ()" method can be used as shown in the code below: *set = {"string1", "string2", "string3", "string4", "string5"}*

set. remove ("string4")

print (set)

Output – {"string1", "string2", "string3", *"string5"}*

You can also use the "discard ( )" method to delete specific items from a Set, as shown in the example below:

set = {"string1", "string2", "string3", "string4", "string5"}

set. discard ("string3")

print (set)

Output – {"string1", "string2", "string4", "string5"}

The "pop ( )" method can be used to selectively delete only the last item of a Set. It must be noted here that since the Python Sets are unordered, any item that the system deems as the last item will be removed. As a result, the output of this method will be the item that has been removed.

set = {"string1", "string2", "string3", "string4", "string5"}

A = set.pop ( )

print (A)

print (set)

Output –

String2

{"string1", "string3", "string4", "string5"}

To delete the entire Set, the "del" keyword can be used, as shown below.

set = {"string1", "string2", "string3", "string4", "string5"}

delete set

print (set)

Output – name 'set' is not defined

To delete all the items from the Set without deleting the variable itself, the "clear ()" method can be used, as shown below: *set =*
{"string1", "string2", "string3", "string4", "string5"}

set.clear ( )

print (set)

Output – set ( )

You can join multiple Sets with the use of the "union ( )" method. The output of this method will be a new set that contains all items from both the sets. You can also use the "update ( )" method to insert all the items from one set into another without creating a new Set.

Set1 = {"string1", "string2", "string3", "string4", "string5"}

Set2 = {15, 25, 35, 45, 55}

Set3 = Set1.union (Set2)

print (Set3)

Output – {"string1", 15, "string2", 25, "string3", 35, "string4", 45, "string5", 55}

Set1 = {"string1", "string2", "string3", "string4", "string5"}

Set2 = {15, 25, 35, 45, 55}

Set1.update (Set2)

print (Set1)

Output – {25, "string1", 15, "string4",55, "string2", 35, "string3", 45, "string5"}

You can also use the "set ( )" constructor to create a Set, as shown in the example below:

Set1 = set (("string1", "string2", "string3", "string4", "string5"))

print (Set1)

Output – {"string3", "string5", "string2", "string4", "string1"}

Exercise

Create a Set "Veg" with string data values as "pies, cake, bread, scone, cookies" and add new items "tart", "custard" and "waffles" to this Set.

Use Your Discretion Here And Write Your Code First

Now, check your code against the correct code below:

Veg = {"pies", "cake", "bread", "scone", "cookies"}

Veg.update (["tart", "custard", "waffles"])

print (Veg)

Output – {"pies", "custard", "scone", "cake", "bread", "waffles", "cookies", "tart"}

Exercise

Create a Set "Veg" with string data values as "pies, cake, bread, scone, cookies", then delete the last item from this Set.

Use Your Discretion Here And Write Your Code First

Now, check your code against the correct code below:

Veg = {"pies", "cake", "bread", "scone", "cookies"}

X = Veg.pop ( )

print (X)

print (Veg)

Output –

bread

{"pies", "scone", "cake", "cookies"}

Exercise

Create a Set "Veg" with string data values as "pies, cake, bread, scone, cookies" and another Set "Veg2" with items as "tart, eggs, custard, waffles". Then combine both these Sets to create a third new Set.

Use Your Discretion Here And Write Your Code First

Now, check your code against the correct code below:

Veg = {"pies", "cake", "bread", "scone", "cookies"}

Veg2 = {"tart", "eggos", "custard", "waffles"}

AllVeg = Veg.union (Veg2) #this Set name may vary as it has not been defined in the exercise

print (AllVeg)

Output – {"pies", "custard", "scone", "cake", "eggos", "bread", "waffles", "cookies", "tart"}

Functions

We began with almost no prior knowledge about Python except for a clue that it was some kind of programming language that is in great demand these days. Now, look at you; creating simple programs, executing codes, and fixing small-scale problems on your own. Not bad at all!

However, learning always comes to a point where things can get rather trickier.

In quite a similar fashion, Functions are docile looking things; you call them when you need to get something done. But did you know that these functions have so much going on at the back? Imagine every function as a mini-program. It is also written by programmers like us to carry out specific things without having to write lines and lines of codes. You only do it once, save it as a function, and then just call the function where it is applicable or needed.

The time has come for us to dive into a complex world of functions where we don't just learn how to use them effectively, but we also look into what goes on behind these functions, and how we can come up with our very own personalized function. This will be slightly challenging, but I promise, there are more references that you will enjoy keeping the momentum going.

Understanding Functions Better

Functions are like containers that store lines and lines of codes within themselves, just like a variable that contains one specific value. There are two types of functions we get to deal with within Python. The first ones are built-in or predefined, the others are custom-made or user-created functions.

Either way, each function has a specific task that it can carry out. The code that is written before creating any function is what gives that function identity and a task. Now, the function knows what it needs to do whenever it is called in. When we began our journey, we wrote "I made it!" on the console as our first program? We used our first function there as well: the print() function. Functions are generally identified by parentheses that follow the name of the function. Within these parentheses, we pass arguments called parameters. Some functions accept a certain kind of parenthesis while others accept different ones.Let us look a little deeper and see how functions greatly help us reduce our work and better organize our codes. Imagine, we have a program that runs during live streaming of an event. The purpose of the program is to provide our users with a customized greeting. Imagine just how many times you would need to write the same code again and again if there were quite a few users who decide to join your stream. With functions, you can cut down on your work easily.

To create a function, we first need to 'define' the same. That is where a keyword called 'def' comes along. When you start typing 'def' Python immediately knows you are about to define a function. You will see the color of the three letters change to orange (if using PyCharm as your IDE). That is another sign of confirmation that Python knows what you are about to do.

def say_hi():

Here, say_hi is the name I have decided to go with, you can choose any that you prefer. Remember, keep your name descriptive so that it is understandable and easy to read for anyone. After you have named your function, follow it up with parentheses. Lastly, add the friendly old colon to let Python know we are about to add a block of code. Press enter to start a new indented line.

Now, we shall print out two statements for every user who will join the stream.

print("Hello there!")

print('Welcome to My Live Stream!')

After this, give two lines of space to take away those wiggly lines that appear the minute you start typing something else. Now, to have this printed out easily, just call the function by typing its name and run the program. In our case, it would be: *say_hi()*

Output:

Hello there!

Welcome to My Live Stream!

See how easily this can work for us in the future? We do not have to repeat this over and over again. Let's make this function a little more interesting by giving it a parameter. Right at the top line, where it says "def say_hi()"? Let us add a parameter here. Type in the word 'name' as a parameter within the parenthesis. Now, the word should be greyed out to confirm that Python has understood the same as a parameter.

Now, you can use this to your advantage and further personalize the greetings to something like this:

```
def say_hi(name):

    print(f"Hello there, {user}!")

    print('Welcome to My Live Stream!')

user = input("Please enter your name to begin: ")

say_hi(user)
```

The output would now ask the user regarding their name. This will then be stored into a variable called user. Since this is a string value, say_hi() should be able to accept this easily. If you pass 'user' as an argument, we get this as an output: *Please enter your name to begin: Johnny*

Hello there, Johnny!

Welcome to My Live Stream!

Now that's more like it! Personalized to perfection. We can add as many lines as we want, the function will continue to update itself and provide greetings to various users with different names. There may be times where you may need more than just the user's first name. You might want to inquire about the last name of the user as well. To add to that, add this to the first line and follow the same accordingly: *def say_hi(first_name, last_name):*

```
    print(f"Hello there, {first_name} {last_name}!")

    print('Welcome to My Live Stream!')
```

first_name = input("Enter your first name: ")

last_name = input("Enter your last name: ")

say_hi(first_name, last_name)

Now, the program will begin by asking the user for their first name, followed by the last name. Once that is sorted, the program will provide a personalized greeting with both the first and last names.

However, these are positional arguments, meaning that each value you input is in order. If you were to change the positions of the names for John Doe, Doe will become the first name and John will become the last name. You may wish to remain a little careful about that.

Hopefully, now you have a good idea of what functions are and how you can access and create them. Now, we will jump towards a more complex front of 'return' statements.

"Wait! There's more?"

Well, I could have explained this earlier, but back then, when we were discussing statements, you may not have understood it completely. Since we have covered all the bases, it is appropriate enough for us to see exactly what these are and how these gel along with functions.

Return Statement

Return statements are useful when you wish to create functions whose sole job is to return some values. These could be for users or programmers alike.

It is a lot easier if we do this instead of talking about theories, so let's jump back to our PyCharm and create another function. Let us start by defining a function called 'cube' which will multiply the number by itself three times. However, since we want Python to return a value, we will use the following code: *def cube(number):*

return number number number

By typing 'return' you are informing Python that you wish for it to return a value to you that can later be stored in a variable or used elsewhere. It is pretty much like the input() function where a user enters something and it gets returned to us.

```
def cube(number):

return number number number

number = int(input("Enter the number: "))

print(cube(number))
```

Go ahead and try out the code to see how it works. We don't need to define such functions. You can create your complex functions that convert kilos into pounds, miles into kilometers, or even carry out far greater and more complex jobs. The only limit is your imagination. The more you practice, the more you explore. With that said, it is time to say goodbye to the world of functions and head into the advanced territories of Python. By now, you already have all you need to know to start writing your codes.

Random function in Python

Start IDLE.

Navigate to the File menu and click New Window.

Type the following:

import math

print(random.shuffle_num(11, 21)) y=['f','g','h','m']

print(random.pick(y))

random.anypic(y)

print(y)

print(your_pick.random())

CHAPTER 5:

OPERATION IN PYTHON

The Python Operators

The Python operators are going to be pretty diverse and can do a lot of different things in your code based on how you use them.

When we are talking about the operators, there are going to be quite a few different types that you can work within the code. Let's explore a bit more about these operators and how we can use these for our needs as well.

Arithmetic Operators

The first type of operator that we are going to take a look at is the arithmetic operators. These are going to be similar to the signals and signs that we would use when we do mathematical equations. You can work with the addition, subtraction, multiplication, and division symbols to do the same kinds of actions on the different parts of the code that you are working with. These are common when you want to do something like add two parts of the code together with one another. You have the freedom to add in as many of these to your code as you would like, and you can even put more than one type in the same statement. Just remember that you need to work with the rules of operation and do these in the right order to make it work the way that you would like. Otherwise, you will be able to add in as many of these to the same code as you need to make it work.

Let's suppose we have two variables whose values are x = 16, y = 4.

Operator	Description of the operator	*Example*
Addition (+)	**This operator will be adding the values on both sides of operands.**	x + y = 20
Subtraction (-)	**This operator will be subtracting the right-hand side value from the left-hand side value of the operand.**	x – y = 12

Multiplication (*)	This operator will be multiplying the two values on both sides of the operands.	x * y = 64
Division (/)	This operator will be dividing the left-hand side value by the right-hand side value of the operand.	x / y = 4
Modulus (%)	This operator will be dividing the left-hand side value by the right-hand side value of the operand and returns the remainder.	x % y = 0
Exponent (**)	This operator will be doing the 'exponential power' calculation on operands.	x ** y = 16 to the power 4
Floor division (//)	This operator will be dividing the operands, the quotient of a number which is divided by 2 is the result.	13 // 3 = 4, simultaneously 13.0 // 3.0 = 4.0;

The above is going to be some of the different operators that you can work with that fit into this category.

Working with these will ensure that we can handle the work and that we will be able to use it inside of our codes.

Comparison Operators

After looking at the arithmetic operators, it is also possible for us to work with the comparison operators. These comparison operators are going to be good to work with because they will let you take over two, and sometimes more, values and statements in the code and then see how they are going to compare to one another. This is one that we will use often for a lot of codes that are going to rely on Boolean expressions because it ensures that the answer you get back will be false and true. So, your statements in this situation are going to be the same as each other, or they will be different. Let's take two variables having the values a = 20, b = 15:

Operator	Description of the operator	*Example*
(==)	This condition becomes true only if two given values (operands) are equal.	(a == b) ⍰ not true
(!=)	This condition becomes true only if the two operands aren't equal.	(a != b) ⍰ true
(>)	This condition becomes true only if the left operand is greater than the right operand.	(a > b) ⍰ true
(<)	This condition becomes true only if the right operand is greater than the left operand.	(a < b) ⍰ not true
(>=)	This condition becomes true only if the left operand is greater than or equal to the right operator.	(a >= b) ⍰ true
(<=)	This condition becomes true only if the right operand is greater than or equal to the left operand.	(a <= b) ⍰ not true

There are a lot of times when we are going to be able to work with these comparison operators to get the most out of the programming that we are doing. You need to consider these ahead of time and make sure that we are going to be able to get the results that we need in our code.

Logical Operators

Next, we are going to be looking at the logical operators. These may not be used as often as the other options, but it is still some time for us to look it over. These operators are going to be used when it is time to evaluate the input that a user can present to us, with any of the conditions that you can set in your code. There are going to be three types of logical operators that we can work with, and some of the examples that you are going to use to work with this in your code include:

And: if x ends up being the false one, the compiler is going to evaluate it. If x ends up being true, it will move on and evaluate y.

Not: if it ends up being false, the compiler is going to return True. But if x ends up being true, the program will return false.

A	B	A AND B	A OR B	NOT
False	False	False	False	True
False	True	False	True	True
True	False	False	True	False
True	True	True	True	False

The chart above is going to show us a bit more about the logical operators that we can work with as well. This can give us a good idea of what is going to happen when we use each of the operators for our own needs as well.

Assignment Operators

And the final type of operator that we are going to take a look at is the assignment operator. This is going to be the kind of operator that will show up, and if you take a look at some of the different codes that we have already taken a look at in this guidebook, you will be able to see them quite a bit. This is because the assignment operator is simply going to be an equal sign, where you will assign a value over to a variable throughout the code. These kinds of operators are used to assign several values to the variables. Let's check the different types of assignment operators.

Operator	Description of the operator	Example
Equal (=)	*This operator will assign values from right side operand to left side operand.*	c = a + b;
Add AND (+=)	*This operator will add the right operand with left operand and assigns the sum to the left operand.*	c += a ⍰ it is equivalent to c = c + a;
Subtract AND (-=)	*This operator will subtract the right operand from the left operand and*	c -= a ⍰ it is equivalent to c = c - a;

	assigns the subtraction to the left operand.	
Multiply AND (*=)	*This operator will multiply the right and left operand and assigns the multiplication to the left operand.*	c = a ⍰ it is equivalent to c = c a;
Divide AND (/=)	*This operator will divide the left operand with the right operand and assigns division to the left operand.*	c = a ⍰ it's equivalent to c = ca;
Modulus AND (%=)	*This operator takes modulus by using both sides' operand and assigns the outcome to left operand.*	c %= a ⍰ it's equivalent to c = c % a;
Exponent AND (**=)	*Does 'to the power' calculation and assigns the outcome to the left operand.*	c **= a ⍰ it's equivalent to c = c**a
Floor division AND (//=)	*It does floor division and assigns the outcome to the left operand.*	c //= a ⍰ it's equivalent to c = c // a;

So, if you are looking to assign the number 100 over to one of your variables, you would just need to put the equal sign there between them. This can be used with any kind of variable and value that you are using in your code, and you should already have some familiarity with getting this done ahead of time. It is also possible for you to go through and take several values, assigning them to the same variable if that is best for your code. As long as you have this assignment operator, or the equal sign, in between it, you will be able to add in as many values over to the variable that you would like.

Working with these operators is a simple thing to work with, but you will find that they show up in your coding regularly. You can use them to add your variables together, to use other mathematical operators, to assign a value over to the variable, or even a few values to your same variable. And you can even take these operators to compare two or more parts of the code at the same time and see if they are the same or not. As we can already see, there are so many things that we will be able to do when it comes to using these operators.

CLASSES

Definition of a Class

The keyword def is used to define a class in Python. The first string in a Python class is used to describe the class even though it is not always needed.

Example

Start IDLE.

Navigate to the File menu and click New Window.

Type the following:

class Dog

'''Briefly taking about class Dog using this docstring'''

 Pass

Example 2

Start IDLE.

Navigate to the File menu and click New Window.

Type the following:

Class Bright:

"My other class"

b=10

def salute(self):

print('Welcome')

print(Bright.b)

print(Bright.salute)

print(Bright._*doc*_)

Classes and Objects in Python

Python supports different programming approaches as it is a multi-paradigm.

An object in Python has an attribute and behavior.

It is essential to understand objects and classes when studying machine learning using Python object-oriented programming language.

Example

Car as an object:

Attributes: color, mileage, model, age Behavior: reverse, speed, turn, roll, stop, start.

Class

It is a template for creating an object.

Example

class Car:

Note

By convention, we write the class name with the first letter as uppercase.

A class name is in singular form by convention.

Syntax

class Name_of_Class:

From a class, we can construct objects by simply making an instance of the class. The class_name() operator creates an object by assigning the object to the empty method.

Class or Object Instantiation

From our class Car, we can have several objects such as a first car, second care, or SUVs.

Example

Start IDLE.

Navigate to the File menu and click New Window.

Type the following:

my_car=Car()

pass

Assignment

a. Create a class and an object for students.

b. Create a class and an object for the hospital.

c. Create a class and an object for a bank.

d. Create a class and an object for a police department.

Example

Start IDLE.

Navigate to the File menu and click New Window.

Type the following:

class Car:

category="Personal Automobile"

def _init_(self, model, insurance): self.model = model self.insurance =insurance   subaru=Car("Subaru","Insured") toyota=Car("Toyota","Uninsured")   print("Subaru   is   a {}".format(subaru._class_.car))   print("Toyota   is   a {}".format(toyota._class_.car))   print("{}   is {}".format(subaru.model,   subaru.insurance))   print("{}   is {}".format(toyota.model, toyota.insurance))

Data Encapsulation/Data Hiding

Encapsulation in Python Object Oriented Programming approach is meant to help prevent data from direct modification. Private attributes in Python are denoted using a single or double underscore as a prefix.

Example

Start IDLE.

Navigate to the File menu and click New Window.

Type the following:

"__" or "_".

class Tv:

def _init_(self): self.__Finalprice = 800

def offer(self): print("Offering Price: {}".format(self.__finalprice))
def set_final_price(self, offer): self.__finalprice = offer t = Tv()

t.offer()

t.__finalprice = 950

t.offer()

using setter function

t.setFinalPrice(990)

t.sell()

Explanation

The program defined a class Tv and used *init*(0 methods to hold the final offering price of the TV. Along the way, we attempted to change the price but could not manage. The reason for the inability to change is because Python treated the _finalprice as private attributes.

The only way to modify this value was through using a setter function, setMaxPrice() that takes price as a parameter.

Polymorphism

In Python, polymorphism refers to the ability to use a shared interface for several data types.

Start IDLE.

Navigate to the File menu and click New Window.

Type the following:

Explanation

The program above has defined two classes Tilapia and Shark all of which share the method jump() even though they have different functions.

By creating a common interface jumping_test() we allowed polymorphism in the program above.

We then passed objects bonny and biggie in the jumping_test() function.

Assignment

a. In a doctor consultation room suggest the class and objects in a programming context.

b. In a football team, suggest programming classes and objects.

c. In a grocery store, suggest programming classes and objects.

Creating an Object in Python

Example from the previous class Open the previous program file with class Bright student1=Bright()

Explanation

The last program will create object student1, a new instance. The attributes of objects can be accessed via the specific object name prefix. The attributes can be a method or data including the matching class functions. In other terms, Bright.salute is a function object and student1.salute will be a method object.

Example

Start IDLE.

Navigate to the File menu and click New Window.

Type the following:

class Bright:

"Another class again!"

c = 20

def salute(self): print('Hello') student2 = Bright()

print(Bright.salute)

print(student2.salute)

student2.salute()

Explanation

You invoked the student2.salute() despite the parameter 'self' and it still worked without placing arguments. The reason for this phenomenon is because each time an object calls its method, the object itself is passed as the first argument. The implication is that student2.salute() translates into student2.salute(student2). It is the reason for the 'self; name.

Constructors

Start IDLE.

Navigate to the File menu and click New Window.

Type the following:

```
class NumberComplex

class ComplexNumber:

 def _init_(self,realnum = 0,i = 0): self.real = realnum
self.imaginarynum       =       i       def       getData(self):
print("{0}+{1}j".format(self.realnumber,self.imaginarynum))
complex1 = NumberComplex(2,3) complex1.getData()

complex2 = NumberComplex(5) complex2.attribute = 10

print((complex2.realnumber,         complex2.imaginarynumber,
complex2.attribute)) complex1.attribute
```

Deleting Objects and Attributes

The del statement is used to delete attributes of an object at any instance.

Example

Start IDLE.

Navigate to the File menu and click New Window.

Type the following:

complex1 = NumberComplex(2,3) del complex1.imaginarynumber complex1.getData()

del NumberComplex.getData

complex1.getData()

Deleting an Object

Example

Start IDLE.

Navigate to the File menu and click New Window.

Type the following:

complex1=NumberComplex(1,3) del complex1

Explanation

When complex1=NumberComplex(1,3) is done, a new instance of the object gets generated in memory, and the name complex1 ties with it.

The object does not immediately get destroyed as it temporarily stays in memory before the garbage collector purges it from memory.

The purging of the object helps free resources bound to the object and enhances system efficiency.

Garbage destruction Python refers to the automatic destruction of unreferenced objects.

Inheritance in Python

In Python inheritance allows us to specify a class that takes all the functionality from the base class and adds more. It is a powerful feature of OOP.

Syntax

class ParentClass:

 Body of parent class

class ChildClass(ParentClass): Body of derived class

Example

Start IDLE.

Navigate to the File menu and click New Window.

Type the following:

class Rect_mine(Rect_mine): def _init_(self): Shape._init_(self,4) def getArea(self): s1, s2, s3,s4 = self.count_sides perimeter = (s1+s2+s3+s4) area = (s1*s2) print('The rectangle area is:' %area) *Example 2*

r = rect_mine()

r.inputSides()

Type b1 : 4

Type l1 : 8

Type b2 : 4

Type l1: 8

r.dispSides()

Type b1 is 4.0

Type l1 is 8.0

Type b2 is 4.0

Type l1 is 8.0

r.getArea()

Inheritance in Multiple Form

Example

Start IDLE. Navigate to the File menu and click New Window.

Type the following:

MultiInherit is derived from class Parent1 and Parent2.

Multilevel Inheritance

Inheriting from a derived class is called multilevel inheritance.

Example

Start IDLE.

Navigate to the File menu and click New Window.

Type the following:

```
class Parent:
 pass
class Multilevel1(Parent): pass
class Multilevel2(Multilevel1): pass
```

Explanation

Multilevel1 derives from Parent, and Multilevel2 derives from Multilevel1.

Method Resolution Order

Example

Start IDLE. Navigate to the File menu and click New Window.

Type the following:

print(issubclass(list,object))   print(isinstance(6.7,object))
print(isinstance("Welcome",object)) *Explanation*

The specific attribute in a class will be scanned first.

The search will continue into parent classes.

This search does not repeat searching for the same class twice.

The approach or order of searching is sometimes called linearization of multi derived classes in Python.

The Method Resolution Order refers to the rules needed to determine this order.

Operator + Overloading

The *add*() function addition in a class will overload the +.

Example

Start IDLE.

Navigate to the File menu and click New Window.

Type the following:

class Planar:

```
def _init_(self, x_axis= 0, y_axis = 0): self.x_axis = x_axis
self.y_axis = y_axis def __str__(self): return
"({0},{1})".format(self.x_axis,self.y_axis) def _add_(self,z): x_axis
= self.x_axis + z.x_axis y_axis = self.y_axis + z.y_axis return
Planar(x_axis,y_axis)
```

Assignment

a. Print planar1 + planar2 from the example above.

Explanation

When you perform planar1+planar2 in Python, it will call planar.*add*(planar2) and in turn Planar.*add*(planar1, planar2).

Revisit Logical and Comparison Operators

Assignment

a. Given x=8, y=9, write a Python program that uses logical equals to test if x is equal to y.

b. Write a program that evaluates x!=y in Python programming language.

c. Write and run the following program m = True

n = False

print('m and n is',m and n) print('m or n is',m or n)

print('not m is',not n)

d. From the program in c., which program statement(s) evaluates to True, or False.

e. Write and run the following program in Python m1 = 15

n1 = 15

m2 = 'Welcome'

n2 = 'Welcome'

m3 = [11,12,13]

n3 = [11,12,13]

print(m1 is not n1)

print(m2 is n2)

print(m3 is n3)

f. Which program statement(s) generate True or False states in e.

g. Write and run the following program m = 'Welcome'

n = {11:'b',12:'c'}

print('W' in m)

print('Welcome' not in m)

print(10 in n)

127

print('b' in n)

h. Which program statement(s) in g. return True or False states.

The special functions needed for overloading other operators are listed below.

Overloading Comparison Operators

In Python, comparison operators can be overloaded.

Example

Assignment

a. Perform the following to the example above Planar(1,1)

b. Again perform Planar(1,1) in the above example.

c. Finally, perform Planar(1,1) from the above example.

Dictionaries

Dictionaries are data types in the Python programming language that is much similar to a list of certain objects contained in a particular collection. Let us venture into some of the similar characteristics and differences that lists and dictionaries share, so as to get the basic idea of what dictionaries are all about. Similar characteristics of these two data types include: They are both mutable, hence due to any shifting at any particular moment of time, they are dynamic. They are able to change in a way that they are to grow and shrink during any episodes and a dictionary is capable of containing another dictionary in it, and a list is too able to contain another list in it hence concluding that these data types can be nested. The only difference between these two data types comes from how the data values are accessed. Lists are normally accessed by various indexing operations whereas dictionaries are basically accessed by the use of various kinds of keys.

Dictionaries basically consist of some key-value pairs that normally are the key to a specified associated value. We define a dictionary in Python by first enclosing the entire list using curly brackets, placing a full colon that separates the key pairs to the associated value placed, and lastly by using a comma mark in separating the various kinds of key pairs that are available in the dictionary. Another way in which dictionaries can be constructed in the Python world is through the use of dict() function in the program. This one works in a way that the value of the argument in the dict() function consists of the keys and the respective values that have been paired along with it. Kindly remember that square brackets are normally used to contain the key-value pairs in the program in question. Once dictionaries have been defined, it is possible to display its contents where they get displayed just the same way they were defined structurally.

Dictionaries are accessed by specifying its relevant key inside square brackets symbol, and in a case where a certain key does not exist in a particular dictionary, an exception is raised right away as an error made. It is then possible to add a certain entry in a particular dictionary where a new key with its value is assigned in the program. In updating a particular entry, a new value is just assigned to an existing key. During the delete of an entry operation, a del statement is normally used specifying the actual key to delete.

Lastly, methods and various operations are normally implemented in dictionaries so various tasks can be achieved. For example, if a developer has the intention of copying a particular dictionary, he or she is obligated to use the copy() method of the Python programming language.

Some of the other methods include:

Clear method

This method clears all the kinds of elements that are present in the dictionary.

Get method

This one gives the value of the key that has been specified in the dictionary.

From keys

This kind of method gives out a particular number of keys and values from the dictionary.

Keys

Output a list that entails the keys in the dictionary.

Pop

This method removes the elements with the specified keys.

Exercise

Create a Dictionary "Hortons" with items containing keys as "type", "size" and "price" with corresponding values as "cappuccino", "grande" and "4.99".

Then add a new item with the key as "syrup" and value as "hazelnut".

Use Your Discretion Here And Write Your Code First

Now, check your code against the correct code below:

Hortons = {

"type" : "cappuccino",

"size" : "grande",

"price" : 4.99

}

Hortons ["syrup"] = "hazelnut"

print (Hortons)

Output – {"type" : "cappuccino", "size" : "grande", "price" : 4.99, "syrup" : "hazelnut"}

Exercise

Create a Dictionary "Hortons" with items containing keys as "type", "size", and "price" with corresponding values as "cappuccino", "grande" and "4.99".

Then use a function to remove the last added item.

Use Your Discretion Here And Write Your Code First

Now, check your code against the correct code below:

Hortons = {

"type" : "cappuccino",

"size" : "grande",

"price" : 4.99

}

Hortons.popitem ( )

print (Hortons)

Output – {"type" : "cappuccino", "size" : "grande"}

Exercise

Create a Dictionary "Hortons" with the nested dictionary as listed below: Dictionary Name Key Value

Coffee01 name cappuccino

size venti

Coffee02 name frappe

size grande

Coffee03 name macchiato

size small

Use Your Discretion Here And Write Your Code First

Now, check your code against the correct code below:

Hortons = {

"coffee01" : {

"name" : "cappuccino",

"size" : "venti"

},

"coffee02" : {

"name" : "frappe",

"size" : "grande"

},

"coffee03" : {

"name" : "macchiato",

"size" : "small"

}

}

print (Hortons)

Output - {"coffee01" : { "name" : "cappuccino", "size" : "venti"}, "coffee02" : {"name" : "frappe", "size" : "grande"}, "coffee03" : {"name" : "macchiato", "size" : "small"}}

Exercise

Use the "dict ()" function to create a Dictionary "Hortons" with items containing keys as "type", "size" and "price" with corresponding values as "cappuccino", "grande" and "4.99".

Use Your Discretion Here And Write Your Code First

Now, check your code against the correct code below:

Hortons = dict (type = "cappuccino", size = "grande", price = 4.99}

print (Hortons)

Output – {"type" : "cappuccino", "size" : "grande", "price" : 4.99, "syrup" : "hazelnut"}

Handling Your Exceptions

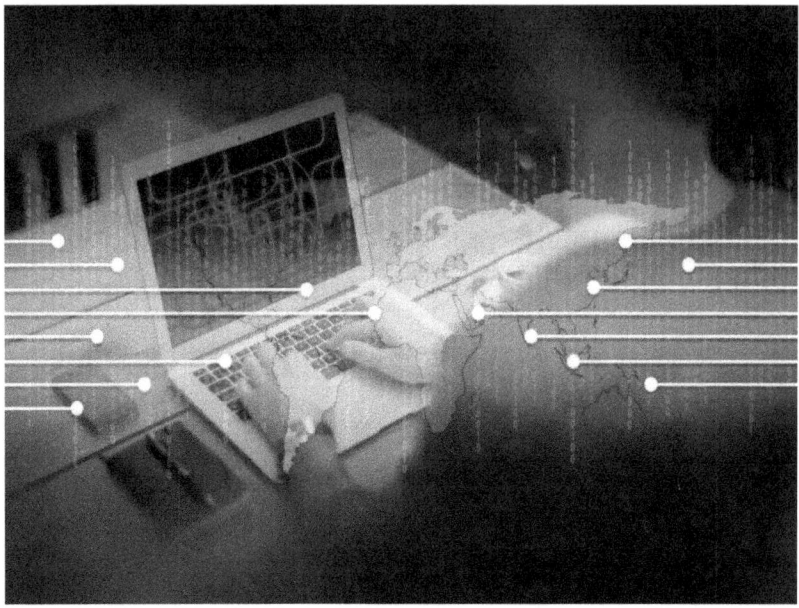

Another great thing that we can do when it comes to working with our Python language is known as exception handling. This is going to be a unique topic that we are going to spend a little bit of time on here because of its importance, but in the beginning, it is going to sound a little bit confusing. Don't worry though because you will catch on quickly, and it won't be long before you can raise an exception, make changes to the exception, and even create some of your exceptions that will be unique to the code that you are working with.

As you are going through some of the work that you need to handle in your code, you may find that there are going to be a few exceptions that the program is already going to bring out for you. And then there are also going to be a few that you will want to write on your own to ensure that the program is going to work the way that you would like. You will be able to find some of the automatic ones already in the standard library for Python. A good example of this is when you or the user will try to divide by zero in the code. The Python language will automatically not allow this to happen, so it is going to raise one of these exceptions for it. But if there is a special kind of exception that you want to work with when you are working on your codes, and you will be able to add this in as well. Now, the first part of this process is to raise an exception that the compiler will be able to recognize because of the standard library of Python. If the user does one of the things that will automatically bring it up the way that we want. This could be something simple like using an improper statement in our code or misspelling one of our classes so that the computer is not sure what you are looking for when you try to search for it at another time. These are things that the compiler is going to see as errors already, and you will need to go through and learn how to handle these. As a programmer, it is going to be your job, and a good idea, to know some of the kinds of exceptions that are going to be found in this kind of standard library with Python. This is going to be helpful to work with because it is going to tell us what to add into our codes, and when an exception is going to turn up for you.

How to Raise an Exception

The first thing that we are going to take a look at here is how to raise an exception inside of your code. We are going to work with some of the automatic ones that are going to show up. When you see these, you want to make sure that you are prepared and that you know what you can do to handle these and ensure that they are easier to work with and understand. If you are working on new code and you notice that there is a potential kind of issue that is showing up, or you want to go through the steps and figure out why your program is doing something that seems a bit off, then you may be able to check with the compiler and see that at this time, it is raising a new exception for you. This is because your program ran a bit, had a chance to take a look through the code, and found that it was not able to proceed. You then have to go through and check it out to figure out what is wrong and how you can fix this kind of issue. The good thing to remember here is that many times the issues you are dealing with will be simple, and you will be able to fix them pretty easily. For example, if you are going through your code and trying to bring up a file, and you provided it with the wrong name, either when you first named it or when it was time to call it up, your compiler is going to go through and raise a new exception. The program took the time to look through your code and noticed that there was stuff going on that it was not able to help you out with at all, and so it raised this exception. A good way for you to get into some of these exceptions and see how they work is to take some time to write out your examples and get some practice with them. This helps us to see what is going to happen when the compiler can raise one of the exceptions.

137

The code that you can use to see what happens with your compiler when you do it is going to be below:

x = 10

y = 10

result = x/y #trying to divide by zero

print(result)

The output that you are going to get when you try to get the interpreter to go through this code would be:

>>>

Traceback (most recent call last):

File "D: \Python34\tt.py", line 3, in <module>

result = x/y

ZeroDivisionError: division by zero

>>>

The picture above is going to be a good example of what is going to show up when we try to divide by zero. We can change up the message to make it work with what we should see within the code.

When you take a look at this example, your compiler is going to bring up an error, simply because you or the user is trying to divide by zero. This is not allowed with the Python code so it will raise that error. Now, if you leave it this way and you run the program exactly how it is, you are going to get a messy error message showing up, something that your user probably won't be able to understand. It makes the code hard to understand, and no one will know what to do next. A better idea is to look at some of the different options that you can add to your code to help prevent some of the mess from before. You want to make sure that the user understands why this exception is being raised, rather than leaving them confused in the process. A different way that you can write out this code to make sure that everyone is on the same page includes:

```
x = 10

y = 0

result = 0

try:

result = x/y

print(result)
```

except ZeroDivisionError:

print("You are trying to divide by zero.")

As you can see, the code that we just put into the compiler is going to be pretty similar to the one that we wrote above. But we did go through and change up the message to show something unless the user raises this exception. When they do get this exception, they will see the message "You are trying to divide by zero" come up on the screen. This isn't a necessary step, but it definitely makes your code easier to use!

How to Define My Exceptions

The next thing that we need to take a look at is some of the steps that we can use to raise our exceptions. With the work that we did above, we spent our time handling any of the automatic exceptions that were found by the program and that the standard library of Python was going to recognize. Then we went a bit further and found out some of the steps that we can use to personalize the message that comes with that exception, rather than just leaving it automatically that most non-programmers, or your regular users, are not going to understand.

Now that we have that out of the way, it is time for us to take our exception writing skills to the next level, and learn how we can write some of our exceptions to fit the kinds of codes that we are writing. This is not going to come into play all of the time, but sometimes it can be helpful to make sure you are going to get everything done the way that you would like.

For example, maybe you are working on some new program or code, and you want to set it up so that your users are only going to be able to add in the input of certain numbers, and then not allow some of the other numbers. Or you could have an exception that will show up when the user tries to guess more than three times. These are both things that could come up in a game, and having the process set up to handle these, and raising some of your exceptions can make a big difference.

Keep in mind with some of these kinds of exceptions that they are unique to the program that you are creating. If you don't specifically add these exceptions into the mix, then the compiler won't recognize that there is anything wrong here, and will just keep going. You can add in as many of these exceptions, and any kind of exception that you would like, and it is going to follow a fairly similar idea to what we say before. The code that we are going to use to ensure that this happens the way that we want though will include:

class CustomException(Exception):

def_init_(self, value):

self.parameter = value

def_str_(self):

return repr(self.parameter)

try:

raise CustomException("This is a CustomError!")

except for CustomException as ex:

print("Caught:", ex.parameter)

When you finish this particular code, you are done successfully adding in your exception. When someone does raise this exception, the message "Caught: This is a CustomError!" will come up on the screen. You can always change the message to show whatever you would like, but this was there as a placeholder to show what we are doing. Take a moment here to add this to the compiler and see what happens.

There are a lot of different times when you will want to work with exception handling. This is something that we are going to focus on more and more when we bring in some of the advanced types of codes that are possible with Python. There are many times that you can work with both types of exceptions that were discussed in this chapter, and you will find that they are going to help you to get more done overall. Make sure to practice some of the codes above to make sure that you have exception handling down and ready to go.

CONCLUSION

E ven though this is the end of this book, I sincerely hope that it is just the beginning of your Python journey. Python has been growing steadily in popularity over the last decade and is increasingly used in all areas of computing. You will find Python powering popular websites such as Pinterest, Instagram, and Reddit. Python is used in scientific computing and is running on supercomputers around the world. It's used for system administration tasks like configuration and package management with YUM and anaconda being prime examples.

Every measure was taken into consideration to ensure that all the chapters give you detailed and easy to understand information. I intentionally used simple language throughout the book to make sure that you get empowered after reading. The book has deliberately avoided sophisticated theories and stuck to simple Explanations that you can use at your convenience when studying.

The thing about computer programming is that your learning will never stop. Even if you think that you have the basics down pat if you don't use what you have learned regularly, believe me when I say that you will soon forget it! Computer programming is evolving on an almost daily basis and it's up to you to keep up with everything that is going on. To that end, you would be well advised to join a few of the Python communities. You will find many of these on the internet and they are places where you can stay up to the minute with changes, where you can join in conversations, discuss code, and ask for help. Eventually, you will be in a position of being able to help the newbies on the scene and it is then that you will realize just how far you have come. So, where do you go from here? The first thing to do is go over this book as many times as necessary to let the content sink in. Don't just read it once and think that you know it all because you don't. The human brain can only take in so much information in one go and it needs time to assimilate that information and store it away before the next influx. Trying to take in pages and pages of code and information will not serve you well and it isn't a case of being the quickest to read it. You can read as much as you like but, once your brain stops taking information in, anything else will be meaningless.

Take your time; do the exercises as many times as you need to until you know that you can write the answers AND understand the answers in your sleep. That is important – it is not enough to know the answers with Python programming. You have to be able to understand WHY the answer is such, the process that gets to that answer if you don't understand the code from start to finish you will never be able to understand the answers.

I hope this book was able to help you to learn the fundamentals of Python Programming quickly and easily and inspire you to create your meaningful programs and practical applications.

The power of programming languages in our digital world cannot be underestimated. People are increasingly reliant on the modern conveniences of smart technology and that momentum will endure for a long time. With all the instructions provided in this book, you are now ready to start developing your own innovative smart tech ideas and turn it into a major tech startup company and guide mankind towards a smarter future.

It is important not to feel like heroes when a program works but above all you should not be depressed when you cannot find a solution to your programming problems. The network is full of sites and blogs where you can always find a solution.

Make it your routine to combine some practical sessions to improve your python programming skills. If you are working with an experienced programmer, follow all the instructions provided to you, and ask questions where you do not understand.

Do whatever you have identified as necessary to improve applications of programming in real life. You will realize that the majority of those who seem to have it all together lack the basic Python programming skills. Try to engage them and teach them a thing or two you have learned herein. You may even recommend or give this book to them.

Good luck.

PYTHON MACHINE LEARNING

The Complete Beginner's Guide to Deep Learning with Python. Learn How to Use Scikit-Learn and Pandas.

WILLARD D. SANDERS

INTRODUCTION

This is a guide that will take you step by step through a wide variety of machine learning concepts and techniques, as well as teach you how to work with complex data. The book is intended for those with an intermediate level of knowledge in working with machine learning algorithms, however, it emphasizes leading you with examples.

Studying machine learning techniques is challenging at times due to some necessity of mathematical as well as programming knowledge, however, this guide aims to demystify this topic and make it easy to understand for everyone. This book places equal focus on teaching theoretical concepts as well as working with real-world applications where you can apply what you learn.

Many people are interested in learning more about machine learning, and in using the Python coding language to help them see the best results. When you are ready to see what machine learning is all about, as well as how you can combine it with your codes and applications to get the best results, then make sure to read through this guidebook to help you get started!

CHAPTER 1:

WHAT IS MACHINE LEARNING

What is Machine Learning?

What is machine learning? It is a particular category of algorithms that allow data scientists to create algorithms that can predict an outcome based on the data it receives. Basically, input data is fed to the software, and then through statistical analysis an output is predicted. These predictions can also be made on new data that is similar to the old data that the machine algorithms already experienced. The purpose is to analyze vast amounts of information, perform comparisons, tests, and come up with a solid conclusion without the need for a data scientist to constantly intervene. This naturally requires the creation of sophisticated machine learning models that are capable of accurately predicting results on their own.

If you have spent any time looking up information about technology and where our world is going now in terms of using computers and programming, then you have likely spent at least a little time hearing about machine learning. Whether you were intrigued by this term or only saw it pop up on some of the articles you were reading, you will find that working with machine learning is a crucial thing to know. It can open the doors to new programming that you can do and can make life easier when developing the software and technology that you want.

If you are new to this arena and haven't spent much time with programming, then you may have never even heard about machine learning. Even so, it is likely that at one point or another, you have used machine learning to help make your life easier. For example, if you have ever done a query on a search engine, such as Google, then it was the technology of machine learning that made this possible. Machine learning is the program that runs these search engine sites and helps you find the results that you want.

Machine learning technology is the only way you will be able to get these programs to work. Regular coding is not able to do this complex task. The system needs to read through your request, look through millions of websites, and then pick out the one that matches up to

153

your needs. And in the beginning, it may not do the best job picking out what you want. But thanks to the machine learning technology behind it, these programs can learn your search preferences and predict exactly what you are looking for based on your choice.

This is one of many examples that shows how we can use machine learning to do some amazing things. Not only can the use of search engines benefit from this technology, but you can use it in many other applications, such as trying to figure out whether to consider a message spam or not.

Unlike some of the conventional programming methods that you may have used in the past, machine learning does not just sit still and give out predetermined outputs. While necessary in some cases, it would not be efficient for a lot of the things we want to do. Unlike the conventional programs, machine learning programs are designed to learn and adapt based on the behavior that the user exhibits. This is excellent because it ensures that the user is going to get the results that they want, rather than being frustrated along the way.

If a computer or another form of technology already has some machine learning capabilities or programs on it, then it can be programmed to form the inputs that the user gives to it. This means that the computer can provide the user with the results, or the answers, that are needed, even if the problem is more complicated. The input for this learning process, which is often known as a learning algorithm will be referred as data training in this process.

How does machine learning work?

With that definition of machine learning in place, the next thing that we need to take a look at is how we can get started with this process. Before we look at all the details that come with machine learning, it is important to first look at the way that the human brain is going to work, and then we can compare that to machine learning to get a better outlook on how all of this should work.

For example, most of us know that when we see a plate that has been heated in the microwave, or we see that there is something that we need to take out of the oven, we know that we should not use our bare hands to touch it. But when we think about it, how do we know that we shouldn't touch something hot?

You will find that machine learning is going to work in a similar manner. At the beginning of the program, the computer has no knowledge. To make the machine able to learn, information needs to be passed over Then with this new information, the machines are able to go through patterns using a variety of techniques to help them out. Over some time, the machines will start to identify patterns out of all the data that they have been able to collect in order to make some good decisions

Training data is often going to be given to the machine ahead of time. These will ensure that you are able to get the program to learn in the manner that it should. The algorithms that you put into this are going to help you learn the models along the way.

Uses of Machine Learning

Machine learning has changed how businesses work and operate in today's world. Through machine learning, large volumes of data can be extracted, which makes it easier for the user to draw predictions from a data set.

There are numerous manual tasks that one cannot complete within a limited time frame if the task includes the analysis of large volumes of data. Machine learning is the solution to such issues. In the modern world, we are overwrought with large volumes of data and information, and there is no way a human being can process all that information. Therefore, there is a need to automate such processes, and machine learning helps with that.

When any analysis or discovery is fully automated, it will become easier to obtain the necessary information from that analysis. This will also help the engineer automate any future processes. The world of business analytics, data science, and big data requires machine learning and deep learning.

Business intelligence and predictive learning are no longer restricted to just large businesses but are accessible to small companies and businesses too.

This allows a small business to utilize the information that it has collected effectively. This section covers some of the applications of machine learning in the real world.

Virtual Personal Assistants

Some examples of virtual assistants are Allo, Google Now, Siri and Alexa. These tools help users access necessary information through voice commands. All you must do is activate the assistant and you can ask the machine any questions you want.

Your personal assistant will look for the necessary information based on your question, and then provide you with an answer. You can also use this assistant to perform regular tasks like setting reminders or alarms. Machine learning is an important part of this tool since it helps the system gather the necessary information to provide you with an answer.

Density Estimation

Machine learning will help a system use any data that is available on the Internet, and it can use that data to predict or suggest some information to users. For example, if you want to purchase a copy of "A Song of Ice and Fire" from a bookstore, and run it through a machine, you can generate a similar copy of the book using that very machine.

Classification

Classification is mainly a type of pattern recognition, and is usually created through a supervised learning method, where the algorithm is taught using a set of data points and properly identified and categorized learning is already available. Classifiers are algorithms that implement the classification method, but the term "classifier" is also used to refer to a mathematical function that directs and categorizes input data into a certain category, but for the purposes of this guide, classifiers are classification method algorithms. Classifiers are usually created by splitting data points into certain variables, which may have various properties, such as categorical properties of blood types *"A -", "O +", "AB +"), ordinal (tall, regular, short), or even integer – valued (such as for spam filters which count for the number of occurrences of particular words). Some other classifiers are built using comparative observation, which have a function that compares distance or similarity between the two.

Clustering

Much like classification, clustering involves grouping together particular data points or observations based on a list of characteristics that would make them belong in the same category. However, clustering tends to be of a broader scope, and less clear – cut as compared to how classification decides to segment its categories. Clusteringor cluster analysis is mostly used by statisticians and data scientists, especially when it comes to solving problems of information retrieval, data compression, or density estimation functions.

As was briefly explained earlier, the clustering function is usually created through an unsupervised machine learning algorithm, as compared to classification functions that are created through supervised learning. This is because clustering does not emphasize specificity as much and works more to gather similar objects together rather than individually define each object into a specific class.

Dimensionality Reduction

Dimensionality reduction is a type of output that tries to reduce the complexity of objects and simplifies the input by mapping them into a lower – dimensional space, which eventually allows the user to simplify the objects and allow them to undergo feature selection or extraction, which is the process of identifying the most relevant attributes, or "features", in order to be better able to build a model. This is useful especially since there tends to be a problem in the increase of available dimensions and as such, sparser relevant data when objects are placed in high – dimensional space. So, dimensionality reduction is often a necessary factor in making objects more accessible and useable.

Regression Analysis

Regression, a word that many people hear and immediately fear due to its complexity, is a statistical process used to estimate and define relationships between and among various variables. Regression refers to multiple techniques that allow us to model the relationship between a dependent variable and one or multiple independent variables, known as predictors. Regression analysis is very useful for helping us understand how the criterion variable, or the dependent variable as it is commonly known, is affected and changes whenever some

159

independent variable changes, while the other independent variables, if any, remain fixed. Regression analysis is also used to help estimate the conditional expectation of the criterion variable given the predictors, so we know what the criterion variable's value the predictors will be once they are fixed.

However, there are also those that use regression analysis to focus on some location parameters of the dependent variable's distribution in relation to the independent variables.

Notably, due to the characteristics of regression analysis, where the data points fluctuate depending on what is being controlled for, the outputs tend to be in a continuous form rather than in a discrete form, matching the changes in real – time.

Latent Variables

When you work with latent variables, the machine will try to identify if these variables are related to other data points and variables within the data set.

This is a handy method when you use a data set where it is difficult to identify the relationship between different variables.

There are times when you will be unable to identify why there is a change in a variable.

The engineer can understand the data better if he or she can look at the different latent variables within the data set.

Advantages and Disadvantages of Machine Learning

Some of the advantages of machine learning are:

When businesses perform analyses, they use large volumes of data, and they prefer using real-time data to perform those analyses. It is difficult for human beings to analyze that volume of data. Therefore, machine learning makes it easier to analyze with ease.

Machine learning is improving day by day. Now that most engineers are integrating machine learning with deep learning, they are reducing the cost of data engineering and data preprocessing.

The disadvantages of machine learning are:

In any machine learning technique, we always train the model using a training data set and then validate that model using a testing data set. The model is then used on newer data sets to predict the outcome. It becomes difficult for one to identify if there is a bias in the model that has been created, and if there is a bias in the model, the inferences made will be incorrect. Social scientists will start relying only on machine learning to solve problems. Therefore, it is important that some improvements and changes should be made to supervised machine learning algorithms to improve the performance of the model.

CHAPTER 2:

ARTIFICIAL INTELLIGENCE AND DEEP LEARNING

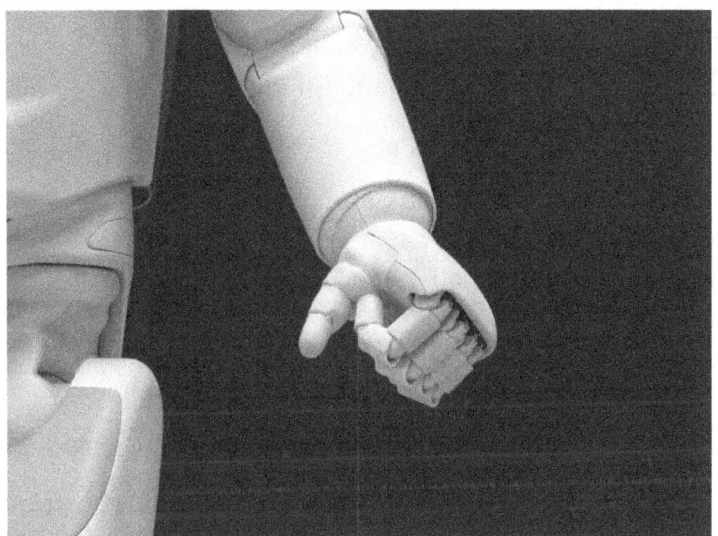

What is deep learning

Deep learning is actually a type of machine learning that is going to be responsible for training our computer on how to perform some of the life tasks that humans do. There are a variety of tasks that could fall into this category, like recognizing speech, identifying what is inside a picture, and making predictions

Instead of organizing the data to run through equations that are already defined, deep learning is going to set up some of the basic parameters that you need for the data, and then will train the computer to learn on its own by being able to see the patterns through many different layers of processing.

Let's dive into this a bit more. Deep learning is important here because it is going to be a foundation of AI, or artificial intelligence, and the current interest that we are seeing in this deep learning is due to how it is related to AI. Deep learning and some of the techniques that come with it have been able to improve the ability of machines to describe, detect, recognize, and classify things in a way that was previously thought to only work for humans.

A good example of this is all of the different things that deep learning is already able to do in our world. many of the algorithms and techniques that work with AIare great at describing the content they look through, detecting objects, and recognizing the speech patterns of those using it, as well as recognizing what is depicted in the images that you present to it. There are many pieces of technology that use this, such as fraud detection, facial recognition, and systems like Cortana and Siri to name a few.

There are already a few developments who are working on advancing what we see with deep learning. Some of these are going to include:

- The improvements that have been done on some of the algorithms have been able to boost up some of the methods that we see with deep learning.

- There are some newer approaches to deep learning that have ensured that the accuracy of the models is going to stay intact.

- There are even some neural networks that have new classes that are developed to fit well for some new applications, including the classification of images and the translation of text.

- There is a ton of information available from companies, much more than there in the past. This helps us to build up new neural networks with a lot of deep layers, including streaming data, physician notes, investigative transcripts, and even some textual data that you could get from social media.

- There are also some computational advances of distributed cloud computing and graphics processing units which can give us all of the computing power that is needed in order to make sure the algorithms for deep learning can actually be done.

At the same time that all of that is going on, the human-to-machine interface that we are used to seeing is changing quite a bit as well.

The keyboard and the mouse that were traditionally used are now being replaced with things like natural language, touch, gesture, and swipe.

This opens up the field to even more AI and deep learning along the way.

This also brings up the question of how deep learning can provide us with a lot of opportunities and applications in the process. A lot of power computationally is going to be needed in order to solve some of the deep learning problems, simply because of the nature of iterations in these algorithms. This results in the complexity going up as the layers increase as well. And you also need to be able to handle a ton of data at the same time in order to get the networks trained and ready to go.

The dynamic nature of the methods of deep learning, and their ability to always adapt and improve to some of the changes in the underlying information pattern, will present us with the information and opportunity that we need to introduce a bit more of the dynamic behavior that is needed into the analytics.

In addition, we can add in a lot more of the personalization that customers want when the analytics comes into play with deep learning. Another great opportunity here is to improve the performance and accuracy of applications, where the neural network is not brand new but has been around for a longer period of time, through better algorithms, and more computing power, resulting in more depth. The next thing that we can focus on is the different ways that you are able to use deep learning to help your business grow and to create great technology that is needed at the same time. To someone who is not all that familiar with how this technology works, it may seem like deep learning is going to be the research phase for computer science and you won't be able to use it that much. However, it is possible to bring in some deep learning in many practical manners to businesses, and it is possible that you are already using quite a few of them today and didn't even notice the technology that is there. Some of the different ways that deep learning is being used today and how we can benefit from it as well will include:

- Speech recognition. Pretty much every industry in our world has seen some sort of use when it comes to speech recognition. If you have ever asked a question to a device, including your phone, to get an answer, then you have used it. Other places like Skype, Xbox, Google Now, and more are using it as well. The deep learning part is brought in because it helps the system to be able to not only recognize when someone is talking to it, but also know what the person is saying or asking as well.

- Natural language processing is another place where deep learning is going to come into play. Neural networks, which are going to be a big component of deep learning, and that we will discuss in more detail later on, have already been used to process and even analyze written texts for a long time. A specialization that comes with text mining, this kind of technique can be used in other places to discover the patterns that are found in places like news reports, the notes that a physician writes out for later, customer complaints, and even more.

- Deep learning can also come into play to help out with recognizing images. One of the more practical applications of this is with automatic image captioning and description of the scenes that are going on. This could be used in a lot of different contexts. One way it is used in law enforcement investigations is to identify some of the criminal activities that are present in the thousands of photos that bystanders in a busy area have submitted. This is just one example though. A self-driving car could also benefit from this kind of technology, so it is able to use its camera from all angles to go in the right direction.

- And the fourth application that we can discuss when it comes to deep learning, although not the last, is going to be the recommendation systems. There are a lot of different companies that are using this, but some common examples of how this would work include Netflix and Amazon. The point of this is to check what you may be the most interested in next, based on the behavior that you have done in the past. Deep learning is going to be used in order to enhance some of the recommendations that happen in environments that are more complex, such as music interests or your preferences of clothing, even when they occur across more than one platform.

There is so much that you can do with deep learning and the world of this kind of programming is bound to keep growing in the future.

Understanding what it is all about and how it can work will make a big difference in the amount of success that you are going to see with it over time as well!

It is through the help of this deep learning that your computer is going to learn how to perform the various classification tasks directly from sound, image, and text. Deep learning models can achieve state-of-the-art accuracy, which in some cases, will be able to exceed the performance that you can get at the human level. Large sets of labeled data and neural network architectures are going to be used to train models with some deep learning.

As you can see, there are a lot of different parts that can come with machine learning. It is a great tool that you can use to get your computer or your system to do some of the things that you may struggle with. For example, machine learning can be used to work with search engines and provide you with recommendations when you are shopping online. And if you need to sort through a large amount of data, machine learning can come into play and help for sure.

What is artificial intelligence?

To help you figure out more about what machine learning and what artificial intelligence are, and how they are different, we are going to look at what AI or artificial intelligence is all about. AI is a term that was first talked about in the 1950s, thanks to John McCarthy. AI was first used to describe a method you can use for manufactured devices to learn how to copy the capabilities of humans in mental tasks.

The term is used a bit differently in our modern world, but the basic ideas are still the same. When you try to implement a program that uses AI, you will enable a machine, such as a computer, to operate and think in the same manner as a human brain can. This is something that is going to benefit you because not only will the AI device be able to think like a human; it can do it in a manner that is more efficient than the human brain can do.

When you are first getting started with these ideas, you may think that AI and machine learning are going to be the same thing. But there are key differences. Some people who don't understand these two terms, and how these terms work may think that they are the same. But often, the way they are being used in the world of programming is what makes them so different and unique.

There are a lot of different activities that computers that hold onto artificial intelligence technology are designed for, and these are going to include things like:

- Planning

- Problem solving

- Learning

- Speech recognition

169

One thing that we can remember when we are working with artificial intelligence is that it is a branch of computer science. In this particular branch, we are going to aim to create machines that are intelligent, and ones that are able to learn and think on their own. In fact, this has become such a prevalent thing in our world that it is known as an essential part of the technology industry, and we are going to see it grow and take off more than ever before.

There has been a lot of research done on artificial intelligence, especially with how much it has risen in popularity over the last few years. This kind of research has been focused and turned into something that is more specialized and highly technical like nothing before. The core problems that come with artificial intelligence are going to be that we need to be able to program a computer for a lot of different traits, and to get it to behave and think in a manner that is almost the same, but faster and more efficient, than we see with a human.

This is going to be complicated, and many programmers, both newer and more advanced, are going to wonder how we are supposed to make this happen at all. And is it really something that we are able to focus on and do, or are we just wasting our time with all of this? You will find that artificial intelligence has really started to take the world by storm, not because it is just a neat theory, but because of all the neat things that it is able to do in the process.

Right now, there are a lot of different ways that artificial intelligence can be used. And some of the things that we are already able to train a computer to do with the help of this technology will include the following:

The ability to move and manipulate any of the objects that you would like.

- Planning
- Problem solving
- Reasoning
- Learning
- Perception
- Knowledge

One of the core parts that you are going to see with some of this research into AI is knowledge. Machines can be trained to act and give off reactions that are like humans, but this is only going to happen if the computer is able to learn off an abundant amount of information that teaches them how the world works. This kind of programming needs to have a lot of information, as well as access to relations, categories, objects, and properties between all the parts so that it can put this to good use and become more knowledgeable.

It is amazing what all of this is able to do if we can work with the technology in the proper manner. When the program or the machine is able to implement some of the artificial intelligence that we are talking about, it will be able to initiate things like common sense, it can start with reasoning and problem solving, and can handle tasks that are really hard to do and kind of tedious, in no time at all.

What does all this mean though? Classification is going to be important here because it is going to help us determine the category where one object is going to belong. And then the regression is going to help us deal with obtaining a set of numerical inputs or outputs to use as examples, which then helps us to discover functions enabling the generation of suitable outputs from the inputs that we are using.

As you can see, there are a lot of different components to talk about when it comes to deep learning and artificial intelligence and learning all of it will take a long time. but understanding some of the basics that we are talking about in this guidebook can help us learn how these technologies are affecting our world, and even how we can use them for our own benefits as well.

CHAPTER 3:

SUPERVISED LEARNING VS UNSUPERVISED LEARNING

Supervised Learning

Supervised learning is a method wherein the computer is fed information, usually in the format of a paired input – output data and uses this information to construct a model that will result in improved predictions or in a more favorable output method. It does this by inferring training data through the given "training examples", which then allows the machine learning algorithm to eventually produce an inferred function using the given examples, that will be used to map more examples and will optimally result in determining the classes of unseen instances, which requires the algorithm to be able to generalize results from the training data to unseen examples in a more reasonable way. Note that the paired teaching data is usually referred to as the "vector" for the input half of the pair, and the output portion is referred to as the "supervisory signal".

Steps in Creating a Flowchart to Solving a Supervised Learning Problem

The first step in creating an algorithm to solve a supervised learning problem is to determine the data type of the training examples to be used. For example, when writing a program in order to conduct handwriting data analysis, the programmer has to decide if they wish to use individual characters, single words, or even entire lines at once in order to train the program. Once the type of data has been determined, the next step is to gather a sufficient sample size of data in order to create the training set to be used for the algorithm. This means that multiple input objects should be gathered, and their expected output counterparts should also be prepared.

Once the training set has been completed, the programmer needs to figure out how exactly they wish their input features to be represented. This means that the input will be converted into a vector, with a number of variables describing it. While it is impossible to perfectly describe the object due to the "curse of dimensionality", the programmer should be able to include a sufficient number of descriptive variables for the computer to have a proper idea of the object. Once this has been completed, the programmer can then determine how they wish their learning function to be structured and how they want to create their algorithm, by using methods such as support vector machines or decision – tree creation, algorithm methods that will be discussed in a later chapter.

Once this has been completed, the programmer can then begin to run the simulation to train their program. Note that certain supervised learning algorithms need a number of control parameters to be determined by the user, and further adjustments may be necessary in order to optimize performance. Once the algorithm has been tested and the program has been trained, the programmer can then try and test their function on a test set different from the training set and check as to whether or not their program is able to come up with the reasonably expected output results.

Curse of Dimensionality

While the "curse of dimensionality" sounds like a very complex concept, and one that comes from a science fiction or fantasy novel, it merely refers to how difficult it is to measure three – dimensional physical objects in the high – dimensional space that data scientists and mathematicians work in, and the various phenomena that arise from this fact. This problem is caused by the fact that as the number of dimensions increases, the volume of the space increases at a rapid pace, so much so that data becomes difficult to gather. One example of how this affects data scientists is the organization of data in high – dimensional space: due to the large amount of data points, many objects look dissimilar though they are similar in reality, which renders many common data organization methods and strategies useless or impractical.

Semi – Supervised Learning

A subset of the supervised learning method, also known as optimal experimental design, it combines elements of supervised learning and unsupervised learning, as unlabeled data entries are included in the training set given to the program. This means that the program learns to calibrate itself through inductive or transudative learning methods, where given the rest of the training set, it infers the proper labels for the unclassified data sets. In fact, the proportion tends to be skewed in favor of unlabeled data sets, with a small portion of the total training set being labeled sets, and the rest being unlabeled data. This can be likened to a math teacher giving worksheets to their students, where the first few problems are already solved, with the solution and answer given, and the rest of the worksheet is left blank. Students learn from the examples and extrapolate the proper method to solve them through the given problems. This method cuts down on costs, as finding or acquiring labeled data is often a resource drain, as it requires a human expert to convert data into a type useable and accessible by a computer. Semi – supervised learning as a method has also been shown to result in higher accuracy in results.

Active Supervised Learning

Active supervised learning is a type of supervised learning where the program is given the ability to actively ask the user questions regarding the label of the data sets. This method uses a combination of labeled and unlabeled data sets, and due to the high cost of manually labeling each data set, the active supervised learning method can be used instead. This allows the computer to attempt to learn using the training set, but if the margin of error in labeling of a particular data set is too high for the program to "tolerate", then the algorithm usually asks the user so that it may properly self – correct. This active participation by a human user is the reason that this method is referred to as the active supervised learning method, and unlike most other methods where little to no human interaction is required once the algorithm starts to run, this method needs a human to be able to fully complete its training set.

Reinforcement Learning

Reinforcement learning is a unique method of supervised learning, in that training sets are not provided. Instead, what happens is that the program is left to carry out actions in an environment, and it learns based on a rewards and incentives method, where if their action is correct, then it is reinforced. This allows the program to find different results, and the focus is taken off of correcting sub – optimal results, but rather finding the method that results in the best performance. This method is often carried out by feedback – intensive activities, such as when playing games against a human user or even driving cars. Reinforcement learning is how some programs such as OpenAI have been able to beat human players in video games, and how Google has been able to develop an autonomous, self – driving car. This learning method often uses the Monte Carlo heuristic method, which allows the computer to calculate probabilities in a resource – starved environment.

Unsupervised Learning

In unsupervised learning, the algorithm is made to parse through totally unlabeled sets of data in order to train itself. This means that there is a higher possibility for errors as compared to the supervised learning method earlier discussed. Unsupervised learning is generally used more for clustering data and values and sees the most use in statistical analysis where there is a need for density estimation functions. Unsupervised learning is more weighted to finding out probabilities of outcomes, such as the probability of Y for any particular X value, and this is why statisticians are the ones that make the most use of this particular machine learning task. However, when it comes to more conventional requirements such as training a program to recognize or predict particular outcomes given a set conditions, it would most likely be more effective to make use of a supervised learning method rather than the unsupervised counterpart.

CHAPTER 4:

HOW TO APPLY MACHINE LEARNING IN THE WORLD

How can I use machine learning?

Collaborative filtering

This is a challenge that a lot of online retailers can run into because they will use it to help them get more profits through sales. Think about when you are on a site like Amazon.com. After you do a few searches, you will then get recommendations for other products that you may want to try out. Amazon uses machine learning to figure out what items you would be interested in, in the hopes of helping you to make another purchase.

Doing translations

There are many times when we will want to take the words that we have and change them to another language. Whether we are taking our native language and translating over to a different language or taking a different language and translating back to our native language, a good translation tool can make a world of difference.

Name identity recognition

This programming is where the computer will need to be able to look at names and such and figure out their entities. It needs to be able to look at the places, actions, and names, out of any document that it comes across. This can be used in a situation where you have a program that needs to digest and then also comprehend a document that you submit to it.

Speech recognition

Another way you can use machine learning is through speech recognition. This can be a hard one to work with because we have to consider the different sounds that each voice has, how the genders sound to one another, the various dialects that each person can use, speech patterns and fluctuations, and even different languages.

The way someone is going to say a word out loud is going to be completely different than the way someone else may decide to use or say it. And the program needs to be able to catch and learn how to recognize these different patterns.

181

Autonomous Vehicles

Machine learning data also fuels autonomous vehicles or self-driving cars. Machine learning techniques have been used before for training autonomous vehicles to steer appropriately when driving on different types of roads.

Top auto executives are also expecting that by 2025, the world will see smart vehicles on the road through machine learning. These are cars capable of not only integrating into the Internet of Things but at the same time, to learn things about its owners and the environment and automatically adjust to it.

Classification of New Astronomical Structures

NASA also uses machine learning to learn general regularities contained in the data within a variety of huge databases. For instance, the space agency uses decision tree learning algorithms to find out how to classify the celestial objects in the second Palomar Observatory Sky Survey.

Data mining algorithms have been used to deal with problems such as star-galaxy separation. Typical surveys have a sheer number of stars and galaxies and separating them needs to be automated. Mixture modeling, DT, ANN, and SOM are some of the common data mining algorithms used for this problem.

Playing Games Like Backgammon

Machine learning algorithms have also been used in the most successful computer programs used for playing games. For instance, TD-Gammon is the world's top backgammon computer program that learned its strategy through the more than one million practice games it played against itself.

Through these practice games, TD-Gammon is able to play at a competitive level of a human world champion. Computer games using machine learning also serve as learning grounds for other applications such as self-driving systems. Games like The Open Racing Car, for example, help train autonomous cars.

Personal Security

If you have attended a big public event before or flown on an airplane, you have likely experienced waiting in a long security line for screening.

Now more than ever, providing your identity has become essential especially in the digital landscape.

To cater to this demand, machine learning and artificial intelligence are rapidly adjusting to help in identity authentication. Machine learning is proving that it can help in eliminating security false alarms. Furthermore, it helps spot things that human screeners might overlook during security screenings.

Data Security

Security in the digital landscape is extremely important as malware continues to be a huge and growing problem. Every day, there are thousands of new malware programs created. To combat these attacks, machine learning is being widely used in a broad range of security applications.

Facial Check with Video, which was developed by Onfido, is one of the latest security applications using machine learning. It encourages users to film themselves performing random movements. This can be used for proving the user's identity by checking the user's facial image.

Healthcare

The use of machine learning allows the processing of more data. It can also better detect more patterns than humans. One example of the advantage of machine learning in healthcare involves a study for computer-assisted diagnosis (CAD).

In the study, the computer was able to detect 52% of the cancers in a review of mammogram scans of women, about a year before they were officially diagnosed.

Using machine learning is also ideal for understanding the risk factors for diseases within large populations.

Fraud Detection

Machine learning is becoming more and more adept at spotting the possible cases of fraud in a wide array of fields. It is also proving to have potential in sweeping the cyberspace and making it a more secure place. It shows many exemplary benefits including tracking of monetary frauds online.

One example of the use of machine learning in fraud detection is the way PayPal uses ML to protect itself from money laundering. The company does this by using a variety of tools to distinguish legitimate or illegitimate transactions by comparing millions of transactions that take place.

Marketing Personalization

Companies also use machine learning in marketing. To better serve their customers and sell well, they need to understand them first. When you browse an online store but do not buy the product, soon you will see digital ads for the same product while surfing the web.

By using your web search info, companies can personalize what ads to show you or which email to send to you.

Machine learning and data mining allow them to know you through the websites you go to or links you click.

All this information helps lead consumers to a sale better than before.

Search engines

Online search is probably the most famous application of machine learning. Google and all the other search engines constantly improve their search engine standards using machine learning methods. They use a machine learning algorithm to learn from your responses.

Recommendations

Surely you are familiar with Netflix, Amazon, and similar services, right? These services also use smart machine learning algorithms to better analyze your activities within their platforms. Upon analyzing and learning about them, the ML algorithm compares it with millions of other users.

This helps online platforms like Netflix to determine what other services or products you might like. These recommendations get better every time you use the platform. Any new data about you will be incorporated and learned by the algorithm to refine its recommendations.

Financial Trading

Many people out there want to be able to predict what will happen to the stock market anytime and any day for apparent reasons.

One way to predict this is the use of machine learning algorithms, which are getting better and closer at cracking stock market changes.

Today, many trading firms are using machine learning systems to predict and perform trades at high volumes and high speeds. Most of these ML systems depend on probabilities that can turn a trade, with significantly low probability but high enough speed and volume, into huge profits.

Natural Language Processing (NLP)

Natural language processing or NLP is being used in varying kinds of interesting applications across disciplines. Together with machine learning, it found great use in the interactions industry as a stand-in for customer service agents.

Using machine learning together with natural language, customer service agents can better and more quickly direct customers to their needed information. One example of machine learning and NLP is a chatbot that can translate and interpret human language input.

Email Spam and Malware Filtering

Email clients use a wide range of spam filtering methods to segregate email spams. To make sure that these spam filters are updated continuously, the filters are powered by machine learning. Typically, rule-based spam filtering is unable to track the latest spam tricks by spammers.

However, machine learning like C 4.5 Decision Tree Induction and Multi-Layer Perception are two of the ML-powered techniques you can use for spam filtering. Besides spam filtering, ML is also great in detecting malware.

Machine learning-powered system security programs can better understand malware's coding patterns. Hence, these security programs are better able to spot new malware showing 2 to 20% variation in their coding patterns. In conclusion, ML-powered security systems are able to offer better protection against malware and email spam

Traffic Predictions

We are commonly using GPS navigation services now to locate and get better directions to our destination. When we use GPS, our current location, as well as velocity, is saved at a central server, which is used for managing traffic.

This information is used for constructing a map of the present traffic. Of course, There is an underlying problem – the number of cars equipped with GPS is considerably low. However, using machine learning in traffic and similar scenarios, it becomes easier to evaluate the areas where there's congestion every day.

In addition to the examples mentioned above, machine learning is proving its potential in more ways. Many people use them and experience ML changing their day-to-day life. Now that you know more about machine learning, you can probably see it in different aspects of your life as well.

Dealing with Big Data

In machine learning, when we refer to big data, we're discussing truly vast amounts of information measured from gigabytes to petabytes. Sometimes the number of zeros that are at the end of a number describing the amount of data just stops making sense to the average person.

The concept isn't new, however. While it was coined at some point during the 90s, the term describes a problem that existed for decades. The concept actually describes quantities of data so huge that traditional forms of data analysis can no longer cope. In other words, when the amount of information pushes the technology of the era to its limits, we can call it big data. There are always points in time when new software had to be coded and new data storing systems had to be built in order to deal with the information appropriately and efficiently.

The Big V's

Nowadays, this concept has evolved to become its very own specialized field within data science and machine learning.

The more modern definition refers to big data as any data that contains a high variety of information coming at an ever-increasing volume and velocity.

This is what sometimes is referred to as the 3 V's in Big Data.

When we talk about volume, we mean the actual amount of data that becomes overwhelming to analyze. Keep in mind that this problem used to exist decades ago, before the arrival of the Internet and the growth of Artificial Intelligence. In a world that is governed by tech, the volume of data can increase only exponentially. Many data scientists have debated on this topic and agreed that roughly every 2 years the volume of data doubles, and the speed doesn't seem to decrease either.

Due to consumer electronics, the velocity at which new data is being created is astonishing. This has led to the development of new ways to deal with data because it either needs to be processed in real time or stored for later processing. Storage space, bandwidth capacity, and computer processing power are all being strained.

Another thing you should keep in mind is that not all data is the same. We aren't dealing with just one format. A large variety of data, whether emails, stock market data, credit card transactions, etc, needs to be stored somewhere, and each storage system needs to be designed specifically for the form of data it needs to hold. This aspect of Big Data creates further complications on top of the storage space problem.

Data is also considered highly valuable under the condition that this value can be extracted. This aspect of Big Data is also heavily influenced by the type of data. If data is not properly structured, it requires a lot of work before it can go into processing. This lower the value of the data, the more unlikely it is to be neatly arranged inside a numeric database.

When looking at recorded Big Data, you should also keep in mind that the quality of it is not equal, usually far from it. The veracity of the data from large datasets has a great impact on how much significance is given to certain information. There are countless reasons why data can be considered or suspected to be inaccurate.

For instance, what if those who collected this data have made assumptions to simply fill in some gaps? What if errors and faulty predictions were introduced in the dataset because of various software bugs? What if the hardware that stored the data suffered from technical abnormalities? Imagine two temperature measurement sensors that record two different values at the exact same time during the same day. Which one is the correct one? When analyzing the data, you can't determine whether one of those temperature sensors was suffering from a glitch or lack of maintenance.

The source of the data can also be suspicious. What if we're looking at a company's data that comes from their social media? There is no way to verify from the gathered data whether that information comes from real users or bots. And let's not forget the impact that human error can have on data. All it takes is one mistake made by a user of an online service when creating his or her account.

As you can see, dealing with Big Data is no easy task. However, the purpose here is to find the valuable bits of information among the

191

noise surrounding it. Governments constantly study such data to improve performance in various sectors. Businesses do the same in order to increase their profits, cut manufacturing costs, and make decisions on creating new brands and products.

Big Data Applications

Let's take a look at some of the areas where Big Data can be used to make a big difference:

Predict demand

Big Data analysis can lead to accurate predictions of a consumer base's demands. We can take in past and present products or services and detect the pattern with the help of machine learning. Finding out the key attributes that made previous products successful can lead us to create new products and services that will have the same potential.

Maintenance

Big Data is used in pretty much all industries, from tool manufacturers to aeronautics. Analyzing vast amounts of data can help data scientists predict when a certain component is going to fail. Information such as manufacturing year, materials, model, and so on can feed algorithms with the right amount of data to make accurate predictions. If such failures are predicted before they happen, maintenance can be called on to solve a problem before it even occurs, therefore significantly reducing the risk of injury or financial loss.

Customer service

We all know that one way or another, businesses record customer information or acquire it from companies specializing in data gathering. Keep in mind that we aren't talking here about social security numbers or credit card information. Remember that last time you visited a certain web store, looked at a couple of items, but didn't buy anything? That data is recorded, and it is valuable. You might think it doesn't mean anything to you, but companies can get a good picture of their consumer base by analyzing every little action they take. Social media, phone calls, website visits and more are all bits of data that is gathered with the purpose of gaining an edge over other companies. Analyzing this Big Data can improve the quality of customer service, products, or reduce negative experiences.

CHAPTER 5:

PYTHON FOR MACHINE LEARNING

Why Use Python for Machine Learning

P ython has certainly become one of the most popular machine languages in the world because it is quite easy to use and very efficient. The simplicity and readability of Python make it easily understandable. Also, it is considered to be one of the most beginner-friendly languages. The vast number of libraries and packages available certainly make it easy to achieve complex functions with minimum coding.

Applications of machine learning usually work with vast data sets and inbuilt libraries like NumPy SciPy, and TensorFlow. All this makes it easy to develop applications for machine learning and deep learning.

Python can also be extended to work for different programs and that's why data scientists are using it to analyze data. Learning to code in Python is a good idea since it will help you analyze and interpret the data to identify solutions that will work efficiently for you. Python can work across various devices and it is designed using clean and simple syntax- thereby making it intuitive and easy to learn for users.

While we are going to take a closer look at the Python coding language and how it works in a bit, it is essential to note here that we are using Python with machine learning because it is one of the best languages for doing this. Python coding is simple, making it easy enough for a beginner to start with, but it still has plenty of power behind it to ensure that you are going to get the work done. The Python language also comes with a big library, it can work well with other languages if you need to have two or more work together, and it is easy to read, even as a beginner.

There are a lot of other coding languages that can work well with machine learning. But often, they add a layer of complications to the process, and they are often saved for those who know that particular language well or some of the most sophisticated options with machine learning.

The Python language is so much better at helping you to complete your tasks. It is simple to work with, easy to understand, and has all the power you need to work with the algorithms in this guidebook. We will even go through some of the algorithms and show you the different Python codes that you can use to get the most out of each one. There is nothing like the ease of use, power, and variety that you can find when you use the Python coding language, even when it comes to machine learning.

Getting Started with python machine learning

Both the Scikit-Learn and the TensorFlow library are going to need to be set up to start with Python machine learning. But the first one that we are going to work with is the Scikit-Learn. This is a library that you can work with if you have Python 2.7 or higher on your system. If those are installed already, then you are ready to go. It is usually best if you are working with machine learning that has one of these newer versions, so installing that can help.

Before you start with installing this library, double check and see if the SciPy and Numpy libraries are installed already —if these are not present, then you need to install them first, and then go through and install the Scikit-Learn.

The installation of these libraries may seem like it is time-consuming; it is essential and you can do this with the help of pip. This pip is a tool that will come along with Python, so you can use the pip as soon as the system is all installed. From here, you can work with the command below to help you get the Scikit-Learn library ready to go:

From here, the installation will be able to run, and then it will complete once all of that is done. It is also possible for you to go through and use the option of conda to help install this library. The command that you will want to use to make sure that this happens is:

conda install scikit-learn

Once you notice that the installation of scikit-learn is complete, it is time to do some importation to get it over to the Python program. This step is necessary to use the algorithms that come with it. The good news is that the command to make this happen is going to be done. You need to go to your command line and type in import sklearn.

If your command can go through without leaving behind an error message, then you know that the installation that you did was successful. After you are done with all of these steps, your scikit-learn library is on the computer, it is compatible with the Python program, and it is going to be ready to use.

Installing TensorFlow

Once you have the Scikit-Learn library put in place in your environment, it is time to start installing the TensorFlow library. When you download this one, you can get a few different APIs for other programming languages outside Python, including Java and C++, so if you need to use these, you can get a hold of them pretty easily. You can download TensorFlow on a few different devices if you would like, but for this guidebook, we are going to discuss how you can install this library on a Windows computer. You can use the pip that we had from before, or Anaconda, to get this downloaded on your Windows computer.

The native pip is often the best way to get TensorFlow installed on your system, without having to worry about the virtual environment that comes with it. But one of the things that you are going to need to keep track of here is that when you install this library with a pip, there are times when this will interfere with some of the other installations of Python that are on the computer, and you need to be aware of this ahead of time.

The good thing to know here is that the only thing that you need to have up and running to make this work is a single command. And once you know this command, TensorFlow can install on your system and be up and running. Once you get this library installed using the pip, you are going to see that there are some options, including the ability to choose which directory you would like to store this on.

Now, you can also choose to install the TensorFlow library on your computer with the help of Anaconda. To do this, you first need to go through and create your virtual environment. You may also want to work with a pip for this one as well. Before you start on this one, make sure that you have a Windows system and Python 3.5 or above. Pip 3 program needs to be in place as well to help with this kind of installation.

Pip is a program that is automatically going to get installed when you get Python on your system. But the Anaconda program isn't. This means that if you would like to make sure that TensorFlow is installed with the use of the Anaconda program, you first need to take the time to install this program. To do this, visit the website for Anaconda, download it from the website, and then find the instructions for installation from that same site.

Once you have gone through and installed the Anaconda program, you should notice that it comes with a package that is called conda. This is a good package to take some time to look at and explore because it will work when you want to manage any installation packages or manage virtual environments. To get access to this package, you need to start up the Anaconda program.

After you get to this point, you can head over to the Windows main screen and then click on the Start menu. You can choose All Programs and expand it out until you see the folder for Anaconda. You click on this prompt to launch the folder. If you need to see what details are in this package, you can run a command in the command line for "conda info." This makes it easier to see the details for that package and the manager as well.

There are a lot of cool things that come with the Anaconda program, but one of the main options that you will want to learn more about will help with machine learning. Anaconda can help you create an environment of Python for your own using this package. The virtual environment is going to be its isolated copy of Python, and it will have the right capabilities of maintaining all of the files that it needs, including the directories and paths. This can be helpful because it allows you to do all of these things while still working with the version of Python that you want and any of the other libraries that you want.

These virtual environments may seem like they are complicated, but they are helpful because they will provide you with a way to isolate your projects and can avoid some of the significant problems that can arise along the way. Note that this is going to be a separate environment compared to the normal Python environment that was downloaded before. This is important because you won't be able to have any effect on the regular Python environment, whether it is bad or good.

At this point, we want to do some work to help us create a virtual environment for that TensorFlow package. This can be done when we use the command of "conda create." Since we want to create a brand-new environment that we have called tensorenviron, we would need to use the formula below to help:

__conda create -n tensorenviron__

At this point, the program is going to ask you whether you would like to allow the process of creating the environment to continue, or if you would like to cancel the work. You will want to type in the "y," and then hit the enter key to move on. This will allow the installation to continue successfully to see the results that you want. Once you have been able to go through this whole thing and create an environment, you will need to take a few minutes and let this environment activate it. If you do not do the activation correctly, you won't be able to use this new environment—you won't be able to get the new environment to work, either. You will be able to activate this using the command discussed earlier. From that point, you will then be able to list out the name that you would like for the environment. An excellent example of what we are talking about here and how it will work includes:

Activate tensorenviron

Now that you have been able to activate the TensorFlow environment, it is time to go ahead and make sure that the package for TensorFlow is going to be installed, too. You can do this by using the command below:

Conda install tensorflow

From here, the computer is going to present you with a list of all of the different packages that you can install together, along with the package for TensorFlow if you would like. You will be prompted to decide if you want to install these packages or not. You can then type in the "y," and hit the enter key on the keyboard.

Once you agree to do this, the installation of this package is going to get started right away. However, notice that this particular process for installation is going to take a bit of time, so you need to wait and remain patient. The speed of your connection will determine the amount of time that the installation process is going to take. The progress and how far the installation has gone and yet to go will be shown on a prompt window. After a certain time, the installation process is going to be complete, and you can then determine if the installation process was successful or not. This is pretty easy to do because you need to run the import statement with Python. The statement is going to be done from the regular terminal of Python. If you are doing this with the Anaconda prompt, you can type in "python" and hit the enter key. This is going to make sure that you end up in the terminal for Python, and from there, you can run the import statement below:

<u>Import tensorflow as tf</u>

If you find that the package wasn't installed properly, you are going to end up with an error message on the screen after you run this code. If you don't see an error message, then you know that the installation of the package was successful.

Python Files

To understand machine learning you are required to understand how files work in Python. The following section discusses Python files.

Files are used for future storage. To read from a file we need to open it and once we are through with it, we have to close it to free the resources.

File Opening

The inbuilt function open() in Python is used to launch a file.

Example

Start IDLE.

Navigate to the File menu and click New Window.

Type the following:

file_name=open("lesson.txt")

file_name=open("D:/Tutorials/lesson.txt")

Exercise

a. Locate a text file on your computer and open using the Python open()

b. Locate a doc/docx file on your computer and open using Python open()

c. Locate an excel file on your computer and open using Python open()

Additionally, appending 'a', write 'w', or read 'r' the file helps indicate the mode when launching the file. The modes are determined by the context and can be changed as the need arises.

Python also allows us to indicate binary or text mode depending on our programming needs. By default, the file is opened in text read mode. Images and non-text files are handled in the binary mode.

Python File Modes

The 'r' is used to launch the file for reading and is the default. The 'w' is preferred when launching writing permissions. For exclusive file creation, we use the 'x' mode. The operation will be unsuccessful if the file we want already exists. The other mode, 'a' is used to launch a file for adding data at the file end while retaining earlier content. For the 't' mode, it will launch the file in default text mode. The 'b' mode is used to launch the file in binary mode. Lastly, the '+' mode is used for launching the file to allow reading and writing.

Exercise

a. Open an existing .txt file on your computer in Python's read mode.

b. Open the same text file in a. in Python's write mode.

c. Open an existing image on your computer in binary mode.

Specifying the File Encoding Type

It is encouraged to specify the file encoding type as it varies from one operating system platform to another and may produce different results if not specified.

Example

Start IDLE.

Navigate to the File menu and click New Window.

Type the following:

```
file_name = open("my text.txt",mode = 'r',encoding = 'utf-8')
```

Closing a File in Python

The method close() is used.

Example

Start IDLE.

Navigate to the File menu and click New Window.

Type the following:

file_name=open("my text.text", encoding='utf-8')

file_name.close()

Exercise

a. Locate a .txt file on your computer, open it using open() and close it using close()

b. Locate a .doc file on your computer, open it using open() and close it using close().

205

Important

This approach will exit without closing a file should an exception occur when performing some operation with the file. We will tackle what an exception is but consider it as an unexpected error during execution of a program. The try..finally block is used to cater for the unseen scenarios when attempting to close a file in Python.

Example

Start IDLE.

Navigate to the File menu and click New Window.

Type the following:

Try:

file_name=open("my text.txt",encoding='utf-8')

finally:

file_name.close()

With this second approach, the user is assured that the file will close properly even if an unexpected error occurs interrupting the program flow.

In this case, the close() method does not have to be explicitly invoked as it is done internally.

Writing to a File in Python

Three modes are used to write into a Python file and they are the 'w'r for writing, 'a' for appending, or 'x' for exclusive creation. The 'w' will overwrite the file and care should be exercised.

Example

Start IDLE.

Navigate to the File menu and click New Window.

Type the following:

```
file_name=open("my text.txt",'w',encoding = 'utf-8')
    file_name.write("In my first file\n")
    file_name.write("Great file\n\n")
    file_name.write("Has three lines\n")
```

Reading a file in Python

In Python, a file must be opened in reading mode to read it. Several methods are available to read a file in Python. If the size parameter is not stipulated, the method will read and return up to the end of the file.

Start IDLE. Navigate to the File menu and click New Window. Type the following:

```
file_name=open("my text.txt",'r'. encoding='utf-8')
file_name.read(5)    # reads the first 5 data

file_name.read(5)    # reads the next 5 data

file_name.read()     # reads till end of file

file_name.read()     # further reading will empty sting
```

Exercise

a. Locate and open a .txt file on your computer using the open() in read mode.

b. In a. read the first three data of the file

c. Read the first five data of the file in a.

d. Read the entire file.

e. Continue reading after reading in d.

Using the for loop when reading a file in Python

The for loop allows us to read a file line after line.

Start IDLE.

Navigate to the File menu and click New Window.

Type the following:

```
file_name=open ("my text.txt",'w'| encoding = 'utf-8')
file_name.write("In my first file\n")
file_name.write("Great file\n\n")
file_name.write("Has three lines\n")
```

We now include the control statement.

```
for line in file_name:
    print(line, end = '')
```

Note

The file has a newline character '\n'. the print() last parameter helps to avoid the creation of two newlines when outputting.

Readline() for Reading Individual File Lines in Python

Example

Start IDLE.

Navigate to the File menu and click New Window.

Type the following:

file_name.readline()

file_name.readline()

file_name.readline()

file_name.readline()

Readlines() Python Method

For the readlines() method, it will scan the entire file lines.

After reading the entire file, the reading method will report empty status.

The reason for empty status is because there are no more arguments for the method to process.

The read() will go through each line in the file until there are no more lines to scan.

Example

Start IDLE.

Navigate to the File menu and click New Window.

Type the following:

```
file_name=open("my text.txt"')

file_name.write("In my first file\n")

file_name.write("Great file\n\n")

file_name.write("Has three lines\n")

file_name.readlines()
```

Exercise

a. Use the readline() method to read each line of a .txt on your computer.

b. Now use the readlines()method to read the entire contents of the .txt in a.

File Methods in Python

These methods enable the user to manipulate files in an easy and efficient manner.

The methods are preloaded, and the user only needs to understand where they can apply.

Method	Description	Method	Description
detach()	Separate the underlying binary buffer from the TextIOBase and return it.	flush()	Flush the write buffer of the file stream.
read(n)	Read at most n characters from the file. Reads till the end of file if it is negative or None.	fileno()	Return an integer number (file descriptor) of the file.
isatty()	Return True if the file stream is interactive.	readable()	Returns True if the file stream can be read from.
readline(n=-1)	Read and return one line from the file. Reads in at most n bytes if specified.	seek(offset,from=SEEK_SET)	Change the file position to offset bytes, in reference to from (start, current, end).
close()	Close an open file. It has no effect if the file is already closed.	readlines(n=-1)	Read and return a list of lines from the file. Reads in at most n bytes/characters if specified.
writable()	Returns True if the file stream can be written to.	tell()	Returns the current file location.
seekable()	Returns True if the file stream supports random access.	truncate(size=None)	Resize the file stream to size bytes. If size is not specified, resize to the current location.
write(s)	Write string s to the file and return the number of characters written.	writelines(lines)	Write a list of lines to the file.

Directory in Python

Python allows us to arrange several files into different directories for easier handling. The collection of files and subdirectories in Python is known as a directory. The os module in Python contains methods for working with directories.

Getting Current Directory in Python

The keyword getcwd() method is used to get the current working directory. The method will return the current working directory in a string form. The getwcwdb()is also used to get a directory.

Changing Directory

The chdir() method helps modify the existing directory. However, the new path we intend to create should be given a string as a method. The path elements can be separated using the backward slash\ or the forward slash/.

Example

Start IDLE.

Navigate to the File menu and click New Window.

Type the following:

os.chdir('C:\\Tutorial')

print(os.getcwd())

Exercise

Use the chdir() to change a directory in the Python root folder on your computer.

Files and List Directories

The listdir() method in Python is used to determine all files and subdirectories within a directory.

The listdir() method accepts a path and gives file lists and subdirectories in that particular path. The listdir() will return from the current working directory if no path is specified.

Example

Start IDLE.

Navigate to the File menu and click New Window.

Type the following:

print(os.getcwd())

C:\Tutorial

os.listdir()

os.listdir('D:\\')

Creating a New Directory

The mkdir() method can be used to create a new directory. The method accepts the path of the new directory and will create a new directory in the current working directory in case the particular path is not defined.

os.mkdir('week2')

os.listdir()

File or a Directory Renaming in Python

In Python, the rename()method is used to rename a file or a directory.

The old name is given as argument 1 and the new name is given as argument 2.

Example

Start IDLE.

Navigate to the File menu and click New Window.

Type the following:

```
os.listdir()
os.rename('week2','fresh_name')
os.listdir(
os.listdir()
```

Exercise

Create a directory using the Python method and name it Lesson. Rename it using a Python method to Python Lessons.

Removing File or Directory in Python

The remove() method is used to delete a file in Python. Likewise, rmdir() is used to remove an empty directory.

Example

Start IDLE. Navigate to the File menu and click New Window.

Type the following:

os.listdir()

['mine_direct']

os.rmdir('mine_direct')

Errors and Exceptions

When the Python interpreter encounters errors, it will raise exceptions. For instance, dividing a number by zero will lead to an exception.

Example of an Error

Start IDLE.

Navigate to the File menu and click New Window.

Type the following:

if y < 3

if y < 3

Runtime errors can still occur when we open a file that does not exist.

A file may not exist because it has been renamed and we are accessing it using the old name or the file has been deleted.

The file could have the same name but has changed the file extension.

Python will create an exception object whenever these runtime error types occur.

Inbuilt Exceptions in Python

Python has several inbuilt exceptions that are flagged when associated errors arise.

The local() method can help list all inbuilt exceptions in Python.

Understanding the Syntax of Python

Having examined how Python runs and executes its program, it is critical to examine the syntax of Python in order to give sufficient information to learners. For the most part, syntax implies the rules of the acceptable ways of arranging words for a particular purpose contained in the series of words. In any case, Python syntax describes how the arrangement of words that characterizes how human users and the framework ought to be composed and interpreted as a Python program. Since you have composed and run your program in Python, intimating yourself with its syntax is an absolute necessity.

The Quotations used in Python Punctuation

In the punctuation of Python, there are bunches of directions done by using the quote. As a matter of fact, Python permits the utilization of quotes to show string literals. Regardless of whether you are using single, twofold, or triple statements, you should begin and end the string with a similar sort to guarantee the program is executed as determined. Note that you'd use the triple statements just when your string keeps running over a few lines.

Declarations Writing in Python

The arrangement of directions given to Python translator to execute and run is called explanation statements. For instance, when you dole out an incentive to a variable, state my variable = "feline", you've recently owned a task expression. Be that as it may, the linguistic structure of a task doesn't live in to that extent or with the citation as task explanation may likewise be as short as c = 3. Different sorts of statements in Python incorporate; if explanations, for statements, while declarations, and some more.

The Language Structure of Multiline Declarations

As examined, declarations are known as guidelines. These directions may be more than a few lines; henceforth multiline declaration. While composing code, you'll have to break a long declaration over various lines. To do this, you may wrap the statement inside enclosures,

217

supports, and sections. In view of styles of composing, this procedure is the favored style for taking care of multiline statements. Then again, there is an approach to wrap different lines by using an oblique punctuation line (\) toward the finish of each line to show line continuation. As you compose your own code, ideal comprehension of the multiline grammar turns out to be simple.

The Sentence Structure of Indentation

For the most part, space is used to indicate squares of code. This is like what is found in other programming dialects like C, C++, and so on as supports. Python is arranged in spaces.

Using Python, squares of codes are arranged by space not by style or inclination but rather as an unbending language prerequisite. Numerous developers have finished up this guideline combined with others which makes Python codes increasingly comprehensible and reasonable. Based on distinguishing proof and structure, a square of code can be effectively recognized when you take a gander at a Python program as they begin a similar separation to one side. If it must be all the more profoundly settled, you can basically indent another square further to one side. For instance, here is a section of a program characterizing the expense of shoes: def cost of shoes ($5):

cost = 5 * $

if 3 >= 15:

cost - = 4

```
elif days >= 2:

cost - = 10

return cost
```

It is important to take note of that; you should dependably ensure that the indent space is steady inside a square. When you use IDLE and different IDEs to include your codes, Python naturally gives space on the consequent line when you enter an explanation that requires space. Space, by the principles of Python, is proportionate to 4 spaces to one side; keep at it.

After the formation of space, you might need to realize how to end it. Simply, the end of each space is the end of the square. The third and last syntactic part that Python expels which could be familiar to most learners of other programming C-like languages is that there is no need to compose anything irrelevant in your code to grammatically access the start and end of a bracketed square of code. You don't need to incorporate start/end, at that point/end if, or surround the bracket square, as you do in C-like language like: if (x > y) {

```
x = 1;

y = 2;

}
```

In Python, rather, you reliably indent every one of the codes in a given single settled square giving it a similar separation to one side. Note that Python uses the codes' physical space to learn where the square begins and stops: If a > b:

a = 1

b = 2

Space implies, now, the clear whitespace around the two settled declarations. Python couldn't care less to what degree you indent (you may use either spaces or tabs), or how you indent; you have the decision of using any number of spaces or tabs. To state, the space of one settled square can be very surprising from that of another. The general language structure decided is just that the majority of the space explanations must be indented a similar separation to one side. This is in such a case that else you will get a grammar mistake, and your code won't keep running until you fix its space to be predictable. Check everything before experiencing the execution arrange.

The Language Structure of Comments

When composing a program, now and then, you'll want to put a few notes just inside your code to give a depiction of what that statement does; such a thing is known as a remark. A remark is most valuable when you need to audit or return to your program for deficiency or change; it is simpler to follow. Also, for different developers who wish to go over your source code, the remark will make it simpler. How you compose and structure remark inside your program is by beginning the line with a hash (#) image. To the Python interpreter, the hash image advises the Python interpreter to disregard the remark when running your code. If your remark is on a multiline, you can use a hash image toward the start of each line. On the other hand, you can likewise wrap multiline remark with triple statements.

The Language Structure of Python Identifiers

Inside the Python program, Python Identifiers are names given to the class, module, function, variable, or different articles. This is any substance you'll be using in Python to compose codes and they ought to be suitably named or given right recognizable proof as they will shape some portion of your program. Here are Python naming shows that you ought to know about: An identifier can be a mix of capitalized letters, lowercase letters, underscores, and digits (0-9). Consequently, coming up next are substantial identifiers: theMovement, my_movement, move_1, and print_what is_world.

Coming up next are exceptional tips on identifiers in Python:

• Within the identifiers, unique characters, for example, %, @, and $ are not allowed.

• Note that 3life isn't legitimate rather life3 is on the grounds that an identifier ought not start with a number.

• Generally, Python is a case-sensitive language. This is commonplace of identifiers and this is the reason the word Happy and glad are two particular identifiers in Python.

• Python keywords can't be used as identifiers.

• When making a class, the Class identifiers must start with a capitalized letter, yet the remainder of the identifiers be lowercase.

• Separation of different words in your identifier is by an underscore.

• You ought to dependably pick identifiers that will sound good to you even after a long hole. This is the reason it is anything but difficult to set your variable to c = 2.

• It is fitting for the future reason that that the more you use a more extended yet progressively important variable name, for example, consider = 2 the easier it becomes at any point of confusion.

Taking everything into account, the syntax of Python has been managed by the 'modules' where you'd need them. This is on the grounds that you will get everything about it independently rather than assembling it. Remember to run the projects as you learn them.

CHAPTER 6:

THE MAIN LIBRARIES TO START MACHINE LEARNING AND WHAT THEY ARE FOR

N ow that we know a bit about the basics that come with the Python language, it is important that we spend some time learning the best libraries and extensions that we are able to add into the mix to make sure that Python is going to work the way that we would like for data science. The regular library that comes with Python can do a lot of amazing things, but it is not going to be able to handle all of the graphing, mathematics, and machine learning that we need with data science.

The good news here though is that there are a few other libraries that we are able to work with that utilize Python and can help with machine learning and data science together. All of these are going to help us handle tasks in a slightly different manner so take a look at them and how they are meant to work with Python and data science. The best libraries that can help you to get this work done will include:

NumPy and SciPy

NumPy. This stands for Numerical Python. The most advanced feature of NumPy is an n-dimensional array. This library has a standard linear algebra function, advanced random number capability, and tools for integration with other low-level programming languages.

SciPy. It is the shorthand for Scientific Python. SciPy is designed on NumPy. It is among the most important libraries for different high-level science and engineering modules such as Linear Algebra, Sparse matrices, and Fourier transform.

If you want to do any kind of work with machine learning or data science with Python, you have to make sure that you work with the NumPy and the SciPy library. Both of these are going to be the basis of many of the other libraries that we are going to talk about here, which is why it is likely that when you work with data science, you are going to also add in a bit of library as well.

First, we will look at NumPy, which is going to stand for Numeric and Scientific Computation. This is a useful library because it is going to lay down some of the basic premises that we need for doing any kind of scientific computing with data science in Python. This library can also help us to get a hold of some functions that have been precompiled for us, and it is fast for handling any numerical and mathematical routine process that you would like to do.

Then there is also the Scientific Python library, which we call SciPy, that goes along with NumPy in many cases. This is the kind of library that you want to work with to add in some kind of competitive edge to what you are doing in machine learning. This happens when you work to enhance some of the useful functions for things like regression and minimization to name a few.

Matplotlib

As you are going through data science and Python, there are going to be times when you will want to work with a graph or a chart or some other kind of visual. This is going to make it easier to see the information that is found in the text, in a glance and the matplotlib will be able to make some of these graphs for you in no time.

The matplotlib extension is going to provide us with all of the parts that we need to take the info and turn it into the visualizations that you need for your data.

This library is going to work with pretty much any of the different types of visualizations that you need from a histogram, bar charts, error charts, line graphs, and more.

Scikit-Learn?

David Cournapeau in 2007 as a Google Summer of Code project developed the Scikit-learn. This process is going to be suitable to use whether you need it commercially or academically.

This is designed for machine learning. It was created on matplotlib, NumPy, and SciPy. This specific library has a lot of efficient tools for machine learning and statistical modeling. That includes regression, classification, clustering, and dimensionality community.

This particular library, has been all done by Python, but some of the different formulas and algorithms that you are going to rely on to make this one work will be written with the help of Cython. If you want to make sure that the performance that you get is the best, you will find that the Scikit-Learn library is the one that you need to focus on. It is especially good at building up some of the models that you need with machine learning. And since it is an open-sourced library, and easy to get started with, you will easily be able to open it up and start using it as soon as needed.

Scikit-learn is an open source Python library. This library is often used to implement different visualization, machine learning, preprocessing, and cross-validation algorithms. This is often done using a unified interface. The functions and features in this package can be used for both data mining and data analysis. These functions include support vector machines, clustering, random forests, gradient boosting, classification, regression, and k-means algorithms.

The Scikit-Learn is the library that we are going to take a look at next. This is a great one to go with when it comes to machine learning. This is because the package that comes with this library is going to provide us with a lot of machine learning algorithms and more that we can use to really get data science to work. It is going to include a lot of different parts that can ensure we analyze the information that is fed into the algorithm in a proper manner.

One other benefit that we are going to see when it comes to this kind of library is that it is easy to distribute, which means it works well in commercial and academic settings, and there are not a lot of dependencies that go with it. The interface is concise and consistent, which makes it easier to work with, and you will find that the most common of the machine learning algorithms are already inside, making it easier to create some of the models you need for data science.

Tensor Flow

This is a framework that you can get through the Google platform, and it is used when you want to create some models in deep learning. This TensorFlow library is often going to rely on some data flow graphs that work on numerical computations. And it can step in and make the process of machine learning easier than before.

You will find that working with TensorFlow makes the process of getting data, of training the models that you would like to use with machine learning, of making predictions, and even modifying some of the results that you see in the future so much easier. Since all of these are going to be important when it comes to machine learning, you can see why we want to spend some time learning TensorFlow.

TensorFlow is a library that the Brain team from Google developed to use on machine learning, and it is especially effective when you want to do some machine learning on a larger scale. TensorFlow is going to bring together algorithms that work with deep learning and machine learning, and it helps to make them more useful through a common metaphor.

Just like what we saw when we were working on the other library, TensorFlow is going to work together well with Python, and it will ensure that you can have a front-end API that can be used when you would like to build a new application. And when you execute these applications, you will see them done in what is known as high-performance C++.

TensorFlow can be used to help with running deep neural networks, for training, building, handwritten digit classifications, recurrent neural networks, word embedding, and even natural language processing to name a few of the neat things you will be able to do.

Both of these two libraries work well with Python, and they are going to do a remarkable job when it comes to ensuring that you are on the right track with your machine learning. Both of these are going to take on a lot of different tasks, and you will need to pick out the right one based on what you would like to get done on your project.

The next thing that we need to work on here is to set up your environment to start with machine learning and see the results that you want. Now that we know a bit more about how all of this works with machine learning and a bit about the Python coding language, it is time to set up the environment so that you can get started. This is a crucial step to take before you try to start on any machine learning and deep learning techniques. And to help you get all of this setup, you need to make sure that your two libraries—Scikit-Learn and TensorFlow—are all set up and ready to get started. TensorFlow, one of the best Python libraries for data science, is a library that was released by Google Brain. It was written out mostly in the language of C++, but it is going to include some bindings in Python, so the performance is not something that you are going to need to worry about. One of the best features that comes with this library is going to be some of the flexible architecture that is found in the mix, which is going to allow the programmer to deploy it with one or more GPUs or CPUs in a desktop, mobile, or server device, while using the same API the whole time. Not many, if any, of the other libraries that we are using in this chapter, will be able to make this kind of claim. This library is also unique in that it was developed by the Google Brain project, and it is not used by many other programmers. However, you do need to spend a bit more time to learn the API compared to some of the other libraries. In just a few minutes, you will find that it is possible to work with this TensorFlow library in order to implement the design of your network, without having to fight through the API as you do with other options.

Pandas

The next library in Python that you want to work with to make machine learning and data science do what you would like. Pandas are going to stand for the Python Data Analysis Library, which helps us to do a lot of the work that is needed in the Python world. This is an open-sourced tool that helps us with some of the data structures that are needed to do data analysis. You can use this library to add in the right tools and data structures to make sure your data analysis is complete, and many industries like to work with this one to help out with some different processes like finance, statistics, engineering, and social science. Best applied in structured data operations and manipulations. It is widely used for data preparation and mining. Pandas were introduced recently to Python and have been very useful in enhancing Python's application in the data scientist community. This Pandas library is going to be really adaptable, which makes it really great for getting a ton of work done in less time. It can also help you work with any kind of data that you are able to bring in, no matter what kind of source you are getting that info from, making it a lot easier to work with. This library is going to come with many different

231

features that you can enjoy and some of the best ones are going to include:

- You can use the Pandas library to help reshape the structures of your data.
- You can use the Pandas library to label series, as well as tabular data, to help us see an automatic alignment.
- You can use the Pandas library to help with heterogeneous indexing of the info and it is also useful when it comes to systematic labeling of the data as well.
- You can use this library because it can hold onto the capabilities of identifying and then fixing any of the data that is missing.

This library provides us with the ability to load and then save data from more than one format. You can easily take some of the data structures that come out of Python and NumPy and convert them into the objects that you need to Pandas objects.

The Keras library

If you are looking for a Python library that can handle data science and data analytics that is also easy for the user to work with, then this is the library for you. It is able to handle a lot of the different processes that come with the other libraries, but it keeps in mind the user, rather than the machine when it comes to designing the interface and the other parts that you use within this coding library. The user experience is easy, the interface is designed to only need a few clicks to get the processes done and it all comes together to make data science and machine learning as easy as possible.

This library is going to work a lot of the modules that are needed for machine learning. You can work with a module that is on its own, or you can combine together a few modules in order to get the results that you would like. There is a lot of flexibility that comes with using this kind of library, and that is one of the many reasons that so many programmers like to use it when completing work with Python data science.

Matplotlib

Matplotlib is basically a Python package that is designed for plotting graphics. It was created because there was little to no integration between the programming language and other tools designed specifically for graphical representations. If you already became familiar with MATLAB, you might notice that the syntax is very similar. That's because this package was heavily influenced by MATLAB and the module we are going to focus on is fully compatible with it. The "matplotlib.pyplot" module will be the core of this basic introduction to visualization. Creating, improving, and enriching your graphical representation is easy with plypot commands, because with this module you can make changes to instantiated figures. Now let's go through some examples and discuss the basic guidelines that will allow you to create your own visualization draft. First, you need to import all the modules and packages by typing the following lines in Python:

- In: import numpy as np

- import matplotlib.pyplot as plt

- import matplotlib as mpl

Now let's start by first drawing a function. This is the most basic visualization, as it requires only a series of x coordinates that are mapped on the y axis. This is known as a *curve representation* because the results are stored in two vectors. Keep in mind that the precision of the visual representation depends on the number of mapping points. The more we have, the higher the precision, so let's take an example with 50 points.

There are going to be a number of toolkits that are available that can help to extend some of the functionality that we are going to see with matplotlib and ensure that we are able to do more with this program in no time at all. Some of these are going to include us going through a separate download, and then others are going to be found with the source code of this library but will have to depend on a few other aspects that are not found in Python or in this library.

Some of the different extensions that we are able to focus on and can really work with when it is time to extend out what matplotlib is able to do will include:

Basemap

This is going to be a map plotting toolkit that can be helpful if this is what you would like to work with inside of your project.

It is a good option to use if you would like to work with political boundaries, coastlines, and even some map projections overall.

Natgrid

This is going to be an interface that goes to the natgrid library. This is best when we want to handle something like the irregular gridding of the spaced data that we have.

Mplot3d

This is going to be helpful when you would like to extend out the 2D functions of matplotlib into something that is more 3D in nature instead.

Excel tools

This library is going to provide us with some of the utilities that we need in order to exchange data with Microsoft Excel if we need it.

Cartopy

This is going to be one of the mapping libraries that we are able to work with that are going to help us with some of the definitions of map projections and some of the arbitrary point, line, polygon, and image transformation capabilities to name a few of the features that we are able to rely on.

There are a lot of different options that we are able to work with along the way in order to handle some of the features of this library. Itt is good for handling most of the features that we would like to see, and most of the graphs that are going to be important when it comes to this kind of data science. For example, you may find that this library works well when we want to handle things like pie charts, line graphs, histograms, bar graphs, area plots, scatter plots, and more.

If you need to create your own chart or graph to go through some of the data that you are handling during this time, then working with the Matplotlib library is going to be one of the best options. It does lack some of the 3D features that you may need, so this is something to consider based on your data. But for some of the basic parts that you would like to add into the mix, and for most of the visuals that you would like to focus on, you will find that the Matplotlib library is going to be able to handle it in no time.

CONCLUSION

Congratulations are in order! You have successfully reached the end of this guide. You have continued with your training and completed the journey of learning intermediate machine learning concepts. You deserve to reward yourself, because data science and machine learning techniques are not easy to grasp, and they can prove to be quite challenging to the uninitiated. Hopefully this book has succeeded in providing you with another stage of knowledge that will allow you to move forward towards the more advanced topics of machine learning. Just keep in mind that you also need to put into practice everything you learn, no matter how difficult it is. Even if you don't fully understand a technique, do more research on your own, experiment with what you know, and more importantly don't give up!

The next step is to get started with some of the coding and all that we have spent time talking about in this guidebook.

There are so many great things that you are able to do when it comes to Python machine learning, and this industry and field is just starting to be explored. Being able to look through some of the different topics that we brought up, and learning how to do some of the work, can make a difference at how well you will be able to utilize this field on your own.

This guidebook explored different aspects of machine learning that you are can do with the help of the Python language. Whether you want to work with supervised learning, unsupervised learning, or even reinforcement learning, you will find that this guidebook has the options that will work for you. We saw how we can break down a lot of different problems and then use the Python coding language to help us get the work done the right way.

The moment you understand programming basics using Python language, it becomes easier to learn machine learning concepts. Machine Learning is essential in everyday life. This book has taken you through many concepts of machine learning. There is no one specific thing that a person can do to learn machine learning overnight. However, if you follow the right steps with dedication and commitment, you will get the results you seek. Combine a number of practical sessions to improve your Python programming skills. If you are working with an experienced Python programmer, follow all the instructions he/she gives you and keep an open communication channel. Get dirty with the IDE and the keyboard.

You might also need to refer to this book at a later date. Keep it and review it as often as you want. Just because you have reached the end of the book does not mean that there is nothing else to learn about Python and Machine Learning. Read more and expand your horizons. It is the only way you will achieve the mastery you seek. Pay attention to Artificial Intelligence particularly because without it, Machine Learning is impossible. Use some of the tips herein to make the world a better place by coming up with your own inventions especially in Artificial Intelligence.

The field of machine learning is growing like crazy. Many computer programmers are interested in learning more about how this works, as well as how they can use it, to see the best results and to help them create new technology into the future.

Keep in mind that in many situations you need to use your own creativity to solve a problem. You need to make the right decisions on which methods to use and what techniques to use in combination with others. Working together with others can ignite that spark and help you find your way towards your goal.

Keep in mind that machine learning is complex, and you need to dedicate a lot of time into researching, analyzing, studying new concepts, and solving problems. This book offers you the tools you need to put the theory into practice and learn how to work with more complex datasets. Keep practicing and never stop learning!

Thank you and all the best!

www.ingramcontent.com/pod-product-compliance
Lightning Source LLC
Chambersburg PA
CBHW072146060526
44654CB00046B/1187